Table of Contents

Introducing Freehand

Graphical images give life and vitality to numerous documents, from newsletters to web pages. Freehand is a powerful drawing program that is equally at home producing graphics for hardcopy publications or on the web. This chapter shows how to obtain and install the program and also details some of the tools and functions that can be accessed.

Covers

Chapter One

What is Freehand 10?

Normally, the naked eye cannot always tell the difference between a vector-based image and a bitmap one. However, when they are enlarged the bitmap becomes pixelated i.e. you begin to see the individual pixels, while the vector image remains smoother.

Freehand is a graphic design program that uses vectors to create images, rather than pixels. Vector-based images are based on mathematical formulas, while images created with pixels (known as bitmap images) are made up of coloured squares. There are two main advantages of vector graphics:

- They can be resized without losing any clarity or detail – the mathematical calculation on which they are based changes, but the quality of the image does not. However, if a bitmap image is resized there is inevitably a loss of quality since the individual pixels have to be stretched to accommodate the new size of the image. In addition, vector-based images can be viewed on any monitor, at any resolution, or be produced on any output device and their quality will remain consistent

- They can be used to create complex images while still retaining a small file size. This is because the images do not consist of the same physical element i.e. dots of colour, as bitmap ones. This is particularly important if the images are going to be imported into web pages, where file size and downloading time can be all important

Despite it being a vector-based graphics program, bitmap images can be used in Freehand. They can either be imported into the program, or existing Freehand graphics can be converted into bitmaps.

Versatility

At a time when online publishing on the web is becoming just as important, if not more so, than hard copy publishing, Freehand acknowledge the importance of both of these mediums. It has facilities for creating graphics for web pages and then exporting them into a suitable format and it can also create web animations for use within a program such as Flash. However, it is just as effective in producing artwork that is going to be printed, either by home users or by commercial printers.

For some links to sites about graphic artists who use Freehand take a look at (no spaces):

www.macromedia.com/ software/freehand/

Freehand is a graphic creation tool that is used by professional graphic artists to produce stunning results. It can also be used by home users who want to create eye-catching artwork for web or desktop publishing output.

Obtaining Freehand 10

Freehand is produced by Macromedia, the market leader in web graphics software. Freehand is their main graphic creation tool and it is integrated closely with Flash, the market leader in web animation. If the graphics created in Freehand are then going to be used on the web, this can be done by importing them into a web authoring program such as Dreamweaver.

Freehand can be purchased from general software retailers, either in person or over the web. It costs approximately £325–£375, depending on where you buy it. Alternatively, it can be downloaded from the Macromedia website at:

- www.macromedia.com/software/freehand

As well as downloading the full product, it is also possible to download a fully-functioning 30-day trial version from the same site.

Freehand can also be bought as a combined studio version with Flash 5. This can be useful if you want to create static or animated graphics in Freehand and then use them in Flash movies. The two programs are very closely integrated and are designed to be used together. The studio package costs approximately £400–£450.

For more information on Flash 5, see 'Flash 5 in easy steps'.

Click here to buy the full functioning version of Freehand

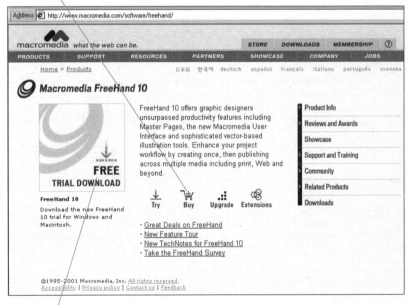

Click here to download the free 30-day trial version of Freehand

Introducing

Installing Freehand 10

If Freehand is downloaded from the Macromedia website it will be loaded automatically onto your computer. If you are using a CD-ROM version it should run automatically on a PC; on a Mac it is activated by double-clicking on the Freehand 10 installer icon. You will then be taken through the installation process and asked to enter information as required. Once the installation has been completed you may be asked to restart your computer.

System requirements
Windows

Once you have installed Freehand, it is a good idea to add a shortcut (Windows) or an alias (Mac) to your desktop. This is done by locating the program file and right-clicking (Windows) or Ctrl+clicking (Mac) and dragging the icon onto the desktop. Release and select Create shortcut here (Windows) or Make Alias (Mac) from the menu.

- Intel Pentium processor or equivalent

- Windows 98, Windows 2000, Windows NT version 4, Windows ME or Windows XP

- 64 Mb RAM

- 70 Mb available hard disk space

- CD-ROM drive

- 800 x 600 pixel resolution, 256-colour display monitor (1024 x 768 resolution and True Colour recommended)

Mac

It is also recommended to have a Postscript Level-2 compatible printer, or later, if you want to print out images from Freehand at a high quality.

- Power Macintosh processor (G3 or higher recommended)

- OS 8.6 or above

- 32 Mb RAM

- 70 MB available hard disk space

- CD-ROM drive

- 800 x 600 pixel resolution, 256-colour display monitor (1024 x 768 resolution and True Colour recommended)

If you are running Freehand on a Mac with 32 Mb of RAM, set the virtual memory to 64 Mb to improve the performance.

First view

The Freehand interface has been designed to match as closely as possible other Macromedia products such as Dreamweaver, Flash and Fireworks. This means you can switch between various programs, while remaining in a familiar environment. When Freehand is first opened there is no document visible. To create a new document:

Dreamweaver is the Macromedia web authoring program and more information can be found out about it in 'Dreamweaver 4 in easy steps'.

Fireworks is an image editing and graphics creation program, primarily for web graphics. For more information, see 'Fireworks 4 in easy steps'.

Select File > New from the menu bar

Once a new document has been created a blank page will be visible in the Freehand environment:

The toolbars and Panels in Freehand are floating, which means they can be dragged around the screen and positioned in different places.

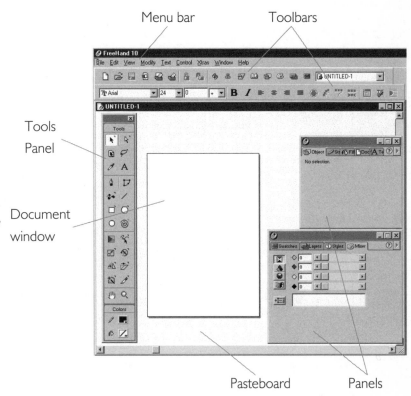

Menu bar   Toolbars

Tools
Panel

Document
window

Pasteboard   Panels

Toolbars

In order to allow maximum editing flexibility, there are eight toolbars in Freehand. This provides a significant amount of design power, but it can be slightly daunting if they are all displayed at the same time. The most commonly used toolbars will be looked at here and the others will be dealt with in the relevant chapters in which their functions occur.

The Menu bar contains all of the commands and functions used within Freehand. The most frequently used of these usually appear on the various toolbars too. The Menu bar commands will be dealt with as they occur in the relevant chapters throughout the book.

Accessing toolbars

To access any of the toolbars the operation is the same:

Select Window> Toolbars and then the required toolbar from the menu bar

Toolbars can be customized to add new buttons or delete ones that are not required. To add a button, select Window>Toolbars>Customize from the Menu bar. In the Customize dialog box, select a button to see its description and drag it onto a specific toolbar to add it.
To remove a button, drag it away from the toolbar on which it is located.

Main toolbar

The main toolbar contains some of the most commonly used editing commands and functions:

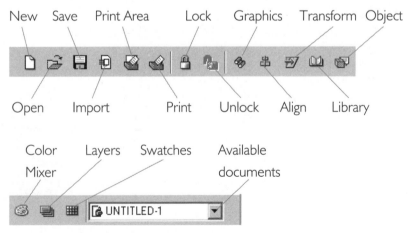

Text toolbar

The Text toolbar contains functions for adding, editing and manipulating text:

Text in Freehand can be manipulated in similar ways to objects. It can be distorted, set to follow a path and be placed inside a pre-set envelope shape. For more information on editing and manipulating text, see Chapter Eight.

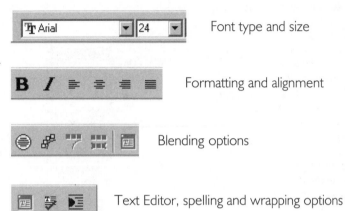

Font type and size

Formatting and alignment

Blending options

Text Editor, spelling and wrapping options

Status toolbar

The Status toolbar gives information about the currently active document, such as magnification settings, number of pages and unit of measurement used:

The unit of measurement used on a page is adopted by the rulers, if they are used. These appear at the top and left of the document window and they can be used for precise positioning of objects.

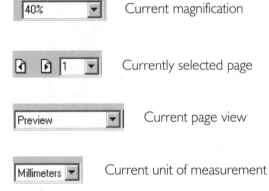

Current magnification

Currently selected page

Current page view

Current unit of measurement

Tools Panel

The Tools Panel contains the most commonly used tools for creating and editing objects. It also allows you to specify the fill and stroke colour for objects. The Tools Panel should be showing by default, but if it is not visible, access it by selecting Window>Tools from the menu bar:

Some of the buttons in the Tools Panel have a small black arrow head at their top right corner. This means that certain preference settings can be used with that tool. Double-click on the arrow head to view the available settings for each tool. For instance, the Rectangle preference settings allow you to specify the degree of curvature for a rectangle.

For more information about using the drawing tools on the Tools Panel, see Chapter Three. For more information on editing objects with the Tools Panel, see Chapter Five.

Items can be added to the Tools Panel by selecting Window> Toolbars>Customize and then dragging items onto the Panel, in the same way as customizing the toolbar.

To remove items from the Tools Panel, drag them away from their current location.

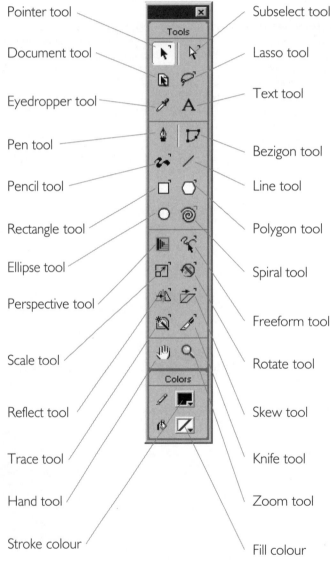

Pointer tool

Document tool

Eyedropper tool

Pen tool

Pencil tool

Rectangle tool

Ellipse tool

Perspective tool

Scale tool

Reflect tool

Trace tool

Hand tool

Stroke colour

Subselect tool

Lasso tool

Text tool

Bezigon tool

Line tool

Polygon tool

Spiral tool

Freeform tool

Rotate tool

Skew tool

Knife tool

Zoom tool

Fill colour

Inspectors

Working with Inspectors

Inspectors are Panels that can be used to create and edit objects. There are five Inspector Panels and they can be accessed by selecting Window>Inspectors from the menu bar. By default they are grouped together. However, it is possible to detach them and position them separately:

To return an Inspector back to the grouped ones, drag its tab until it is positioned over the other Inspectors. When it is released it will automatically snap back into position.

Click on a tab and drag it away to detach it from the other Inspectors

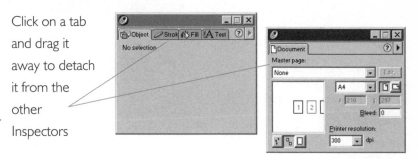

Object Inspector

This displays information about the currently selected object. New values can be entered to change the object's attributes.

Only open Inspectors as you need them. Otherwise the screen may get too cluttered and it will make it harder to work in the document area.

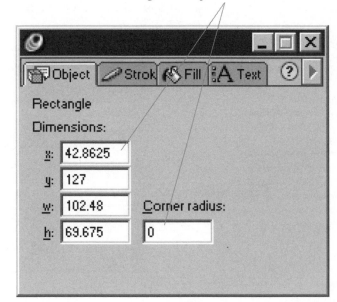

Stroke Inspector

This displays information about the currently selected stroke. New values can be entered to change the stroke attributes.

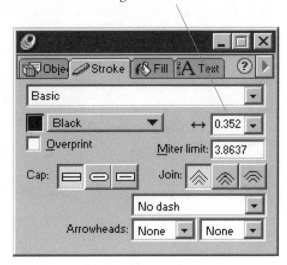

The current stroke and fill are displayed in the Color section of the Tools Panel, underneath the tools themselves.

Fill Inspector

This displays information about the currently selected fill of an object. New values can be entered to change the fill attributes.

When a new stroke or fill is specified, this will become the default for any new objects that are created. This will remain until a new stroke or fill is selected.

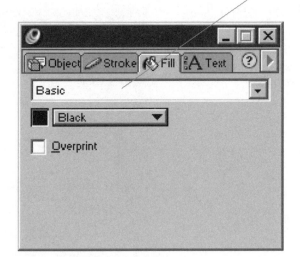

Text Inspector

This displays information about the currently selected piece of text. It can be used to format new or existing text and also to add text effects.

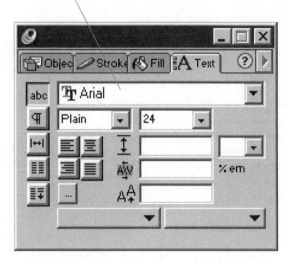

The items covered by the Document Inspector can be specified when a document is first set up. For more information about this, see Chapter Two.

Document Inspector

This displays information about the current document, such as the number of pages and the page orientation.

Freehand documents can consist of one or more pages. This information is displayed in the Document Inspector.

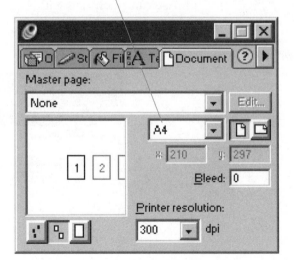

Panels

Working with Panels

Panels are very similar to Inspectors in their appearance and they perform various tasks to do with creating and using colours and also manipulating objects within an image. To access the available Panels:

As with Inspectors, Panels are grouped together by default. To change this they can be dragged away from one another, in the same way as with Inspectors.

Select Window>Panels from the menu bar and then the required Panel

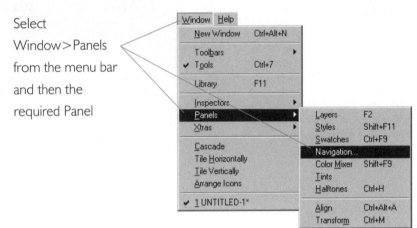

Layers Panel

Layers are a very powerful tool within a Freehand image as they allow parts of an image to be edited individually while still remaining part of the overall graphic.

This allows you to create new layers within an image. Different elements can then be placed in separate layers so that a complex image can be created without too many graphical elements overlapping each other on the same layer. The Layers Panel can also be used to move and delete layers.

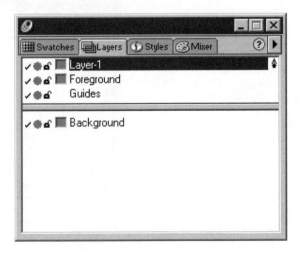

For a more in-depth look at layers, see Chapter Seven.

Styles Panel

This allows you to apply pre-defined styles to graphics and text. This is a commonly used function in word processing programs, where text can have a specific style applied to it, but in Freehand this can also be applied to graphics.

For more information on using styles, see Chapter Seven.

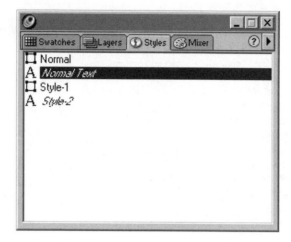

For more information on using colour, see Chapter Six.

Swatches Panel

This can be used to select available colours, including custom ones that have been created. The Swatches Panel can also have new colours added to it.

The Swatches Panel can have colours added to it from professional colour libraries that are available within Freehand. This allows for considerable flexibility when choosing colours for a graphical element within an image.

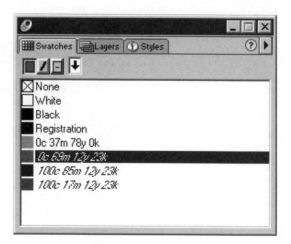

Navigation Panel

This can be used to add hyperlinks to items that are going to serve as navigation points once the graphic has been published on the web. Basic programming actions can also be added from within the Navigation Panel.

If a graphic in Freehand has had navigation and/or actions added to it, it is advisable to then export it into Flash, or into the SWF file format, so that this functionality can be used. This in turn can then be used within an HTML document for publication on the web. The Macromedia web authoring tool, Dreamweaver, is the one that integrates most closely with Freehand and Flash.

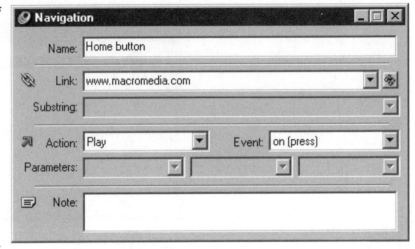

Color Mixer Panel

This can be used to mix your own custom colours. This can be done within four separate colour palettes. Once a new colour has been mixed, it can then be added to the Swatches Panel.

The use of colour is one of the fundamentals of Freehand, so the Panels concerned with this area play a very important part within the program.

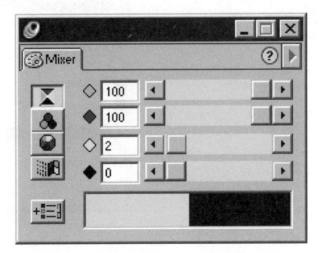

Tints Panel

This is another Panel that is concerned with colour. This one enables you to create colours that are a tint of a base colour. For instance, if a colour has been created in the Color Mixer Panel, it can then be edited in the Tints Panel, so that a new colour is created by reducing the intensity of the original.

In the Tints Panel, new colours can be created by specifying a tint of the base colour as a percentage. This can range from 10–90%, as a solid block, or from 0–100% using the slider control.

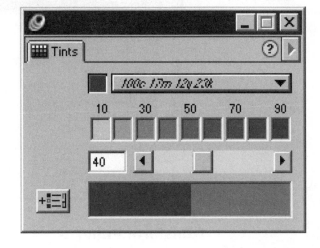

Halftones can be used during the printing process of printing separation. This is when individual colours within a graphic (Cyan, Magenta, Yellow and Black, also known as CMYK) are printed separately in order to create the final effect.

Halftones Panel

This can be used to print selected elements of an image as halftones. This can only be applied to objects of a particular type and it is only really applicable if you are creating graphics for hard copy distribution rather than on the web.

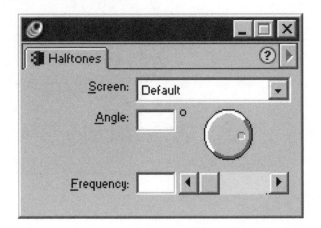

Align Panel

This can be used to align single, or multiple, items on the page. An object has to be selected before it can be positioned using the Align Panel.

To select more than one object at a time, select the Pointer tool, then hold down Shift and click on all of the items to be selected.

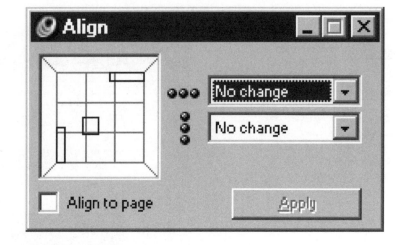

The options on the Transform Panel can also be selected from the Tools Panel. However, the Transform Panel allows for specific values to be entered for each function, unlike selecting them from the Tools Panel.

Transform Panel

This can be used to move, scale, rotate, skew or reflect a selected object, or objects.

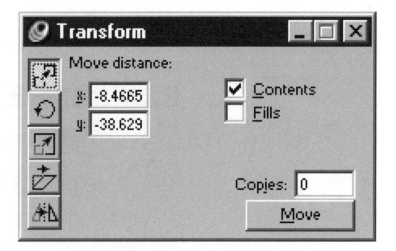

Preferences

There are several preferences dialog boxes available for different functions within Freehand. These are accessed by selecting Edit>Preferences from the menu bar.

Freehand has more preference options than a lot of drawing and graphics programs. Get used to using the program itself first, before worrying too much about the preferences. Once you feel more confident within the Freehand environment, it will be easier to work with the preference options.

Tabs

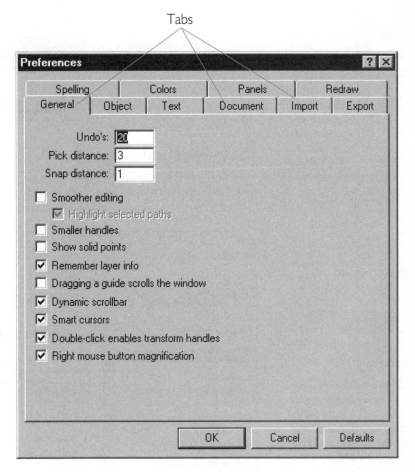

Once a particular preference has been selected, this will act as the default until it is specifically changed.

Some of the Freehand preferences will be looked at as they occur in the relevant chapter. The available groups (tabs) are: General, Spelling, Object, Colors, Text, Panels, Document, Redraw, Import and Export.

Getting help

The Help menu in Freehand is accessed from the menu bar:

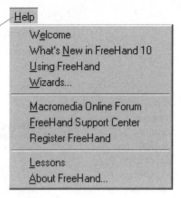

The Wizards options can be used to specify various settings before you start work on a document. This includes creating settings for online graphics and hard copy ones.

Using Freehand

Select the Using Freehand option to access a comprehensive directory of the functions within the program:

Click here to select a topic, which will then be displayed in the main window

The Help options also contain links to the Freehand Help Centre within the Macromedia website. This contains tips, case studies and information about upgrades and new versions of the software. An active connection to the Internet is required to access this.

Lessons and Tutorials

Select the Welcome option to access a menu for either lessons or tutorials. These cover various aspects of Freehand and show how to manipulate graphical elements.

Preparation basics

If the basics of a Freehand document are set up properly it makes the creative process a lot easier. This chapter looks at opening documents, using master pages and also some of the devices that can be used to aid the drawing process.

Covers

Chapter Two

Opening a new document

When a new Freehand document is started the Document Inspector can be used to specify a variety of settings for the new file. Before this can be done, a new file has to be opened, by either selecting File>New from the menu bar or clicking on this button on the Main toolbar:

Once a new file has been opened, it will appear as a blank white page. The Document Inspector can then be accessed to specify the document setup. To do this:

Select Window> Inspectors> Document from the menu bar

The Document Inspector serves the function of the Page Setup or Document Setup commands in other programs.

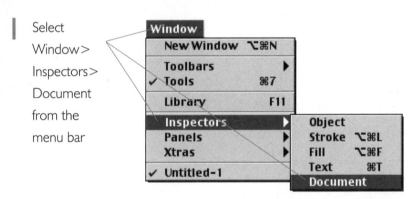

The Document Inspector should be displayed on the page

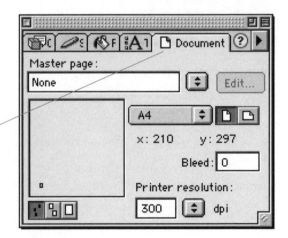

Using the Document Inspector

The Document Inspector can perform several page setup tasks, such as page size, orientation and printer resolution. It can also be used to create master pages, which are pages that contain elements that appear throughout a Freehand document.

Page size

Freehand documents can contain numerous pages and so can be used to produce a variety of artwork within the same file.

To set the size of the page on which you want to output a Freehand document:

Click here on the Document Inspector and select the required paper size

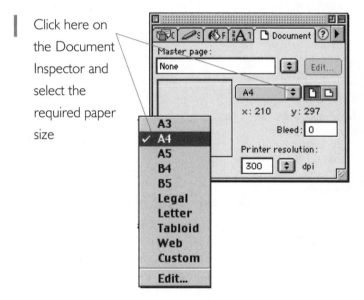

Orientation

Portrait orientation is when the page is at its longest vertically and Landscape is when it is at its longest horizontally.

The orientation of a document determines whether it is laid out in Portrait or Landscape. To specify this:

Click here; select the orientation, which is then displayed here in the thumbnail view

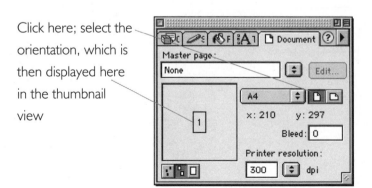

The Bleed setting is a specific value that is the same as the default unit of measurement for the document i.e. if this is millimetres, the bleed setting will be the same. (For how to specify units of measurement, see page 13).

Most consumer desktop printers cannot print to the very edge of an A4 page, regardless of the bleed setting that is applied. However, if the paper size is set to one smaller than A4, then the bleed setting can be used successfully.

To print top quality artwork, you should be looking at a printer with a minimum resolution of 600 dpi and preferably one between 1200–2400 dpi.

The printer resolution settings will only take effect if the printer can print to that standard.

Bleed settings

The bleed setting for a document is a printing term and it determines how far over the edge of the paper the document will go when it is printed. With certain paper sizes, this can usually only be done on a professional printing press. The idea is that the print area should contain the very edge of the paper. To specify this:

Enter a value here

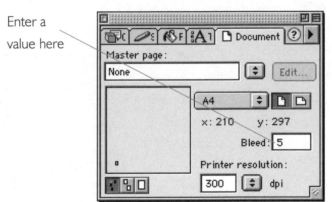

Printer resolution

The printer resolution determines the quality of the document when it is printed. It is measured in dots per inch, and the higher the setting, then the better the final image. However, this is dependant on the printer being able to operate to this level. To set the printer resolution:

Click here and select a value from the drop down list

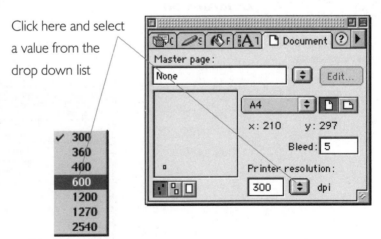

Adding pages

Pages can be added to a Freehand document, either before any content has been added or at any time during the authoring process. To do this with the Document Inspector:

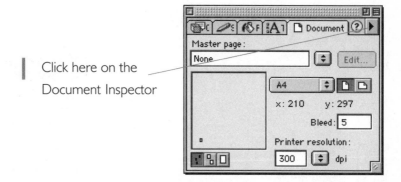

1 Click here on the Document Inspector

Different pages within a Freehand document can have different page properties applied to them. So one page could be A5 size and portrait orientation, while the following one could be A4 size and landscape orientation.

These properties can be edited once they have been set initially in the Document Inspector.

2 Select Add pages from the menu

3 Enter the number of new pages to be added

4 Enter the paper size, orientation and bleed settings for the new pages. Select OK

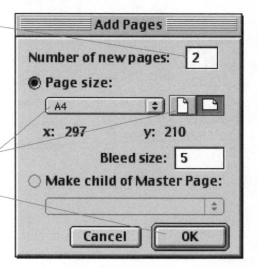

Selecting pages

If a document has been created with a lot of pages it is important to be able to move quickly between them. Two options for doing this are with the Document Inspector and the Go-to-Page pop-up menu.

Document Inspector

Depending on the magnification, it is possible to display more than one page at a time. For more on magnification, see page 50.

1 Select one of the thumbnails to make that page the active one

2 Click here to select the size at which the thumbnails are presented in the Document Inspector

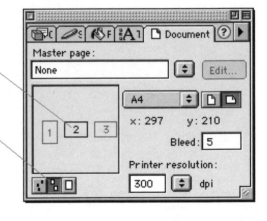

Go-to-Page pop-up menu

The forward and backward arrows located next to the Go-to-Page pop-up menu can be used to move to the pages before and after the currently selected one.

1 Click here on the Status bar (Windows) or the Document window (Mac) and select a page number

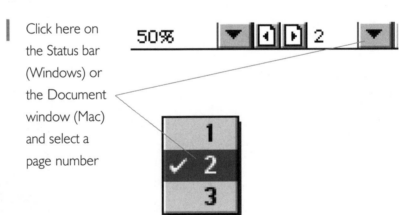

Moving and deleting pages

Moving pages

1 Select a page in the Document Inspector

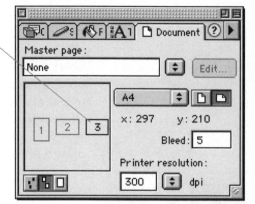

Pages in the Document Inspector can be selected with any tool in the Tools Panel, as long as the correct preference setting is selected. To do this, select Edit>Preferences from the menu bar. In the Preferences dialog box, select the Document tab and check on the box next to Using tools sets the active page.

2 Drag it to its new location. The page number will be updated, as will those for the rest of the pages within the document

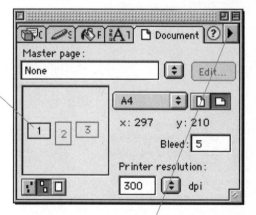

Pages can also be deleted by selecting them with the Page tool on the Tools Panel and then dragging them out of the Document Inspector.

Deleting pages

1 Select a page in the Document Inspector and click here

2 Select Remove from the menu

> **Add pages...**
> **Duplicate**
> **Remove**
>
> **New Master Page**
> **Convert to Master Page**
> Release child page

About master pages

When creating Freehand documents with several pages, it can be useful to be able to use the same elements throughout the document, i.e. a company logo or a header or a footer. This can be done through the use of master pages, created when the document is first opened or at any time during the authoring process. A master page is one that contains elements that can be used to appear on subsequent pages. The elements of a master page can be applied to a single page or throughout an entire document. Several different master pages can also be created and used on different pages throughout a document and standard pages can also be converted into master pages at any time. When working with master pages, both the Document Inspector and the Library can be used.

When a page has a master page applied to it, the page is known as a child page.

Preparing for master pages

Before a master page can be created, either the Document Inspector or the Library has to be visible. They can both be used individually to create master pages, but they can also perform separate tasks in relation to them. The Document Inspector can be accessed as shown on page 26. To access the Library:

The Library is an area for storing items that are going to be used throughout a document, or shared across several documents. It is discussed here specifically in relation to master pages. For a more detailed look at the Library, see Chapter Seven.

| Select Window>Library from the menu bar

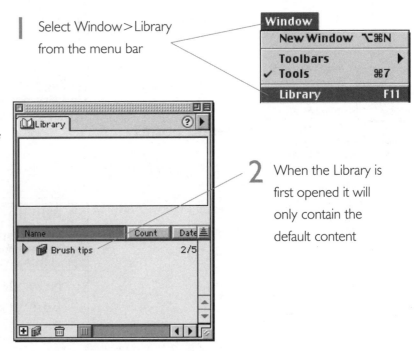

2 When the Library is first opened it will only contain the default content

Creating master pages

Master pages can be created through either the Document Inspector or the Library. In both cases a new document has to have already been opened.

Using the Document Inspector

1 Click here on the Document Inspector and select New Master Page

When a master page is created using the Document Inspector, it is also automatically inserted into the Library.

2 The master page opens up as a new document. Add the content for the master page and then close the document in the normal way for a Windows or Mac file

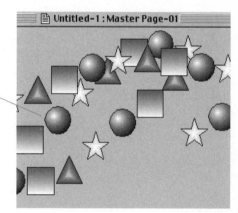

When master pages are created through the Document Inspector they are named Master Page-01 and so on. However, they can be renamed in the Library to give them more meaningful titles (see the HOT TIP on the next page).

3 Click here in the Document Inspector to view the available master pages

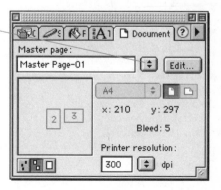

Using the Library

The Library can be used to store a variety of elements that are going to be reused throughout a document. These include graphics, text and even printer registration marks.

1 Click here in the Library and select New Master Page

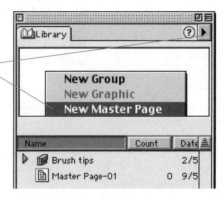

Whatever content is added to a master page will appear whenever that page is applied to a page, or pages, within the document.

2 The master page opens up as a new document. Add the content for the master page and then close the document in the normal way for a Windows or Mac file

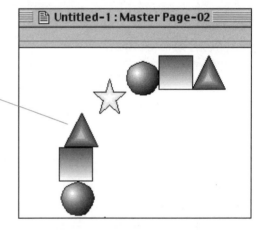

To rename a master page, double-click on it in the file list within the Library. It should then become highlighted in blue with a thin black box around it. Overtype the current name with the new one.

3 Master pages appear in the preview window and in the file list

Applying master pages

As with creating master pages, they can be applied to a document using either the Document Inspector or the Library. In addition, they can also be applied to individual pages within a document, or to the whole document.

When a master page has been applied to a page, or pages, within a document, this can be edited at any time by removing the master page or selecting a different one.

Using the Document Inspector on a single page

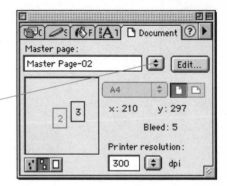

1 In a document that has already had master pages created, click here to select a master document

The content of a master page cannot be edited on a page to which it has been applied. It sits in the background, like a separate document shielded by a pane of glass.

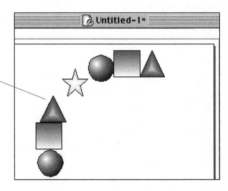

2 The content of the master document appears on the page, which is now known as a child page

The content of a master page can be edited by selecting it in the Document Inspector, clicking on the edit button and then making the changes in the original master page document. The same procedure can be done by selecting the master page in the Library and selecting Edit from the Library menu, which is accessed by clicking the triangle at the top right of the Library.

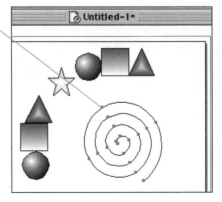

3 Additional content can be added to the page. This only appears on this page – it does not affect the master document and it does not appear on any other pages to which this master page is applied

Using the Library

1 In a document that has already had master pages created, click here to select a master page

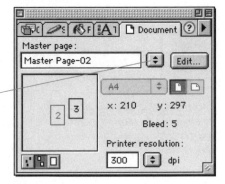

When applying a master page from the Library, it can also be dragged from the file list in the bottom half of the Library.

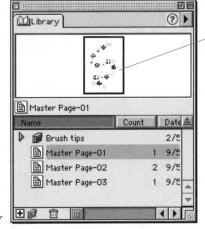

2 Click and drag from here onto the document page

When a new master page is applied to a document page, it overwrites the content of any previously applied master pages. However, it leaves the content of the document itself untouched.

3 The master page is applied to the document page and overwrites any prior master pages that have been applied

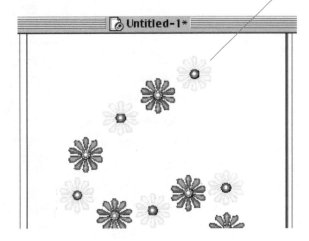

Applying master pages throughout a document

On some occasions it is useful to be able to apply the same elements on every page of a document. This could be a recurring piece of artwork, an address or a design element such as a graphical header and footer. In cases like this it is possible to create the recurring items on a master page and then apply it to the entire document. This can be achieved by using the Document Inspector:

When working with master pages, plan their design and use carefully before they are created and applied. This can save a lot of time and effort later. If they are used well, master pages can be an excellent time-saving device.

1 Create a master page and select it in the Document Inspector

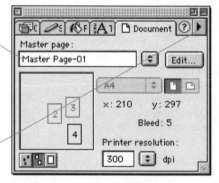

If a master page is edited, the changes take effect on all of the document pages to which the master page has been applied.

2 Click here on the Document Inspector and select Add pages

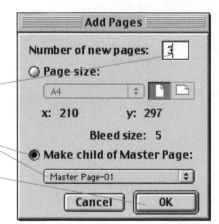

New pages can be added to a document at any time during the authoring process. They can have the same master page applied to them as the rest of the pages within the document or a new one, or none at all. Every page in a document can have a different master page applied to it.

3 Enter the number of pages required for the whole document

4 Check this box on and ensure the right master page is selected. Select OK

Applying separate master pages

Master pages are very versatile and it is possible to use numerous different ones within the same document. This can be done when adding new pages or existing pages can have new master pages applied to them.

Using the Add Pages dialog box

In the Add Pages dialog box the page orientation cannot be changed if it is different from that of the selected master page. A different page orientation can be selected, but at the expense of a master page selection.

1 Once a master page has been applied to a document, select Add Pages from the Document Inspector menu, as shown on the previous page

2 Enter the number of pages and click here to select a different master page from the one that has already been applied

Add Pages

Number of new pages: 4

○ Page size:

A4

x: 210   y: 297

Bleed size: 5

◉ Make child of Master Page:

Master Page-03

Cancel   OK

In order to apply more than one master page within the same document, two or more master pages must first be created, so that there is a choice in the Add Pages dialog box

3 The different pages will appear with the content of the separate master pages

Untitled-1*

Using existing pages

If you have already added pages to a document and applied a master page to them, it is possible to select individual pages and apply different master pages to these separate document pages. To do this:

| Select one of the Document Inspector thumbnails or select a page in the document window

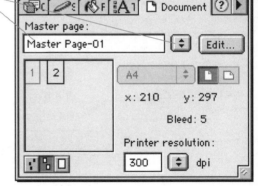

2 The currently selected master page is displayed here

Master pages do not have to be used at all within a document, as elements can be copied and pasted from one page onto another. However, they do ensure that items appear at exactly the same location on different pages.

3 Click here and select a different master page. This will only be applied to the currently selected page. The rest of the pages within the document will still have their original master pages applied to them

Removing master pages

Master pages can be removed from either the Document Inspector or the Library. If they contain content, a warning dialog box will appear before the page is deleted permanently, using the Document Inspector. If the Library is used, a dialog box will ask if you intend to delete all instances.

Using the Document Inspector

1 Select the master page

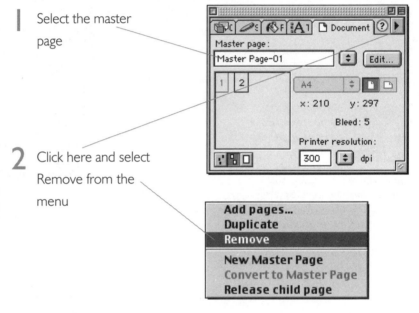

If a master page is removed by mistake, it can be reinstated by selecting Edit>Undo from the menu bar. Depending on what you have done since the master page was removed, you may have to perform this command several times to return to the required point. The number of Undo steps can be specified by selecting Edit>Preferences from the menu bar and entering the required number in the Undo's box under the General tab.

2 Click here and select Remove from the menu

3 If the master page contains content, the following dialog box appears. Select Yes (Windows) or OK (Mac) if you want to delete the master page and all of its content

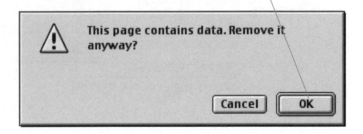

Using the Library

When master pages are deleted using the Library, it is possible to detach the content while removing the actual master page. If this is done, the content takes on the characteristics of simple graphics.

If a master page is removed but the content is released, this can be converted back into a master page by selecting the page and selecting Convert to Master Page from the Document Inspector menu.

1 Select the master page

2 Click here and select Remove from the menu or click on the Wastebasket button

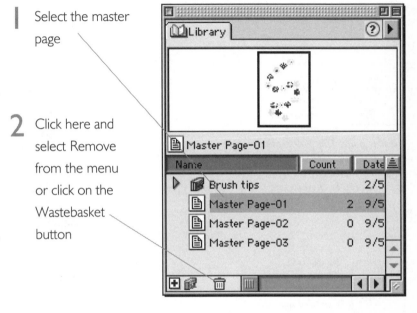

When a master page is created the content becomes symbols. When the master page is applied to a document page, the symbols appear as instances. This means that they are not objects in their own right, but they are references to the original symbol. When a master page is deleted this relationship is broken and the instances revert back to simple graphics.

For more on symbols and instances, see Chapter Seven.

3 In the dialog box, select Release to remove the master page and leave the content in place. Select Delete to remove the master page and all of its content

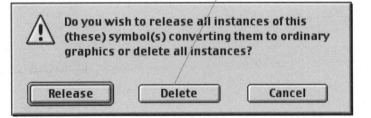

Sharing master pages

Exporting master pages

It is possible to export master pages from one document so they can be used in other publications. Once this has been done, the master page can then be imported into the new document. To export a master page:

Do not use the File>Export command from the menu bar to export a master page. This will export the whole file, rather than a specific master page, even if it is selected in the Library.

By default, Freehand tries to export master pages to a folder within its own directory. It may be easier to navigate to one of your own directories and save it there instead.

1 Select any master page in the Library. Click here and select Export from the menu

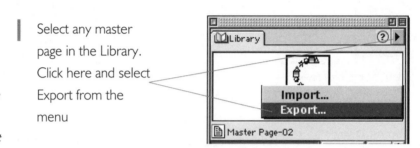

2 Select a master page to export and select Export

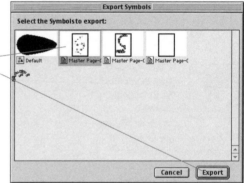

3 Select a location for the exported page and select Save

Importing master pages

Once a master page has been exported, it is can be made available in other documents by using the import command:

Importing master pages can be an excellent time-saving device if similar design elements are being used across several different documents.

1 Click here on the Library and select Import from the menu

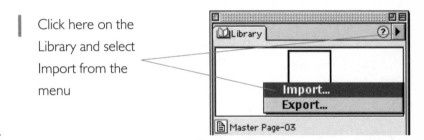

2 Select the file to import and select Open

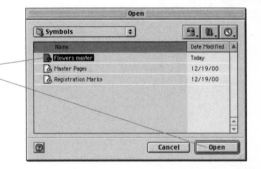

If a page is not selected in the Import Symbols dialog box (step 3) then nothing will be imported into the document.

3 Select a page and select Import. The page will appear in the Library as the next sequentially numbered master page

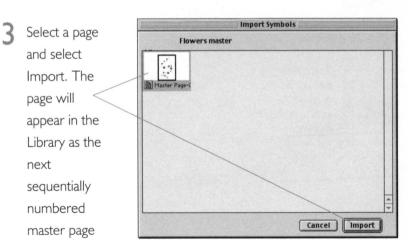

Rulers

Since Freehand can be used to create precision graphics, it is important to be able to measure objects and distances to a high degree of accuracy. One important aid in achieving this is through the use of rulers, which appear at the top and left hand side of a document

Setting the unit of measurement

The unit of measurement used by the rulers can be edited according to the type of work being done. This is done within the Units pop-up box at the bottom of the page:

The unit specified in the Unit pop-up box is used for all measurements within a document, until another one is selected.

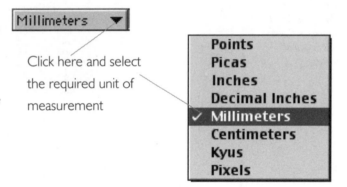

Click here and select the required unit of measurement

Displaying the rulers

By default the rulers are not displayed, but they can be made visible as follows:

The rulers can be used in conjunction with the Object Inspector for determining the exact dimensions of objects.

1 Select View>Page Rulers>Show from the menu bar

2 The rulers display on the page

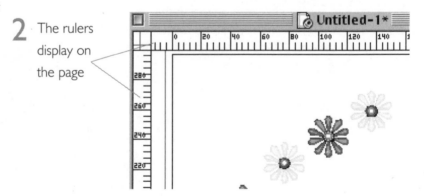

Setting the zero point

When using rulers to position objects on a page, it is usually easiest to do this if the page's zero point (i.e. the co-ordinates of its top left hand corner) is 0,0. This can be set as follows:

Setting the zero point can have important implications for positioning elements on a page. It is always useful to know the exact location of the zero point.

1 With the rulers showing, click on this crosshair

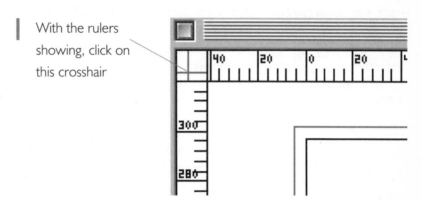

In addition to the units of measurements available in the Units pop-up box, you can create your own custom units. To do this, select View>Page Rulers>Edit from the menu bar. Enter a name for the new unit of measurement, then select the units upon which it is to be based. Select Accept and then Close to add the custom measurement to the Units pop-up box.

2 Drag the crosshair until it is positioned exactly over the top left hand corner of the page. Release the crosshair

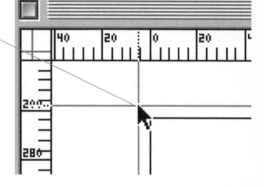

3 The zero point is now located here

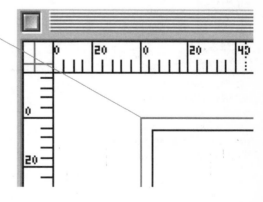

Grids

A grid in Freehand is like drawing on a page of graph paper — it consists of small squares, the sizes of which can be edited, which can be used to create graphics and also to position them.

Showing and editing a grid

A grid can be made visible or hidden, depending on the author's preference. To do this:

Grids can be frequently turned on and off during the authoring process, depending on the task that is being undertaken.

| Select View>Grid>Show from the menu bar

2 The grid is then displayed as horizontal and vertical lines in the document window

The unit of measurement for a grid is the same as the default that has been selected for the current document — this is displayed at the bottom left of the screen.

To edit the size of the grid:

If the Relative Grid box is checked on in the Grid Size dialog box, objects snap to locations within the grid box that are relative to their original position within the box. If the Relative Grid box is checked off, objects snap to the intersection of grids.

| Select View>Grid>Edit from the menu bar

2 Enter a new Grid Size and select OK

Edit Grid

Grid size: 2

☐ Relative grid

Cancel   OK

Snapping to grid

Objects can be made to snap to the nearest available gridlines. This has the effect of pulling the object to the gridline, as if it were magnetised. To do this:

1 Select View>Grid>Snap to Grid from the menu bar. When an object is moved near to the grid, it will be snapped so that it lies on top of the nearest gridline

If Snap to Grid has been selected, this will operate even if the grid is hidden.

Snapping options

Preferences can be set to determine the proximity, in pixels, that an object has to be to a gridline in order for it to snap to it. To do this:

1 Select Edit>Preferences from the menu bar

2 Select the General tab and enter a value in the Snap distance box. Select OK

The maximum value for the Snap distance is 5. If a higher value is entered, it is automatically overwritten with 5.

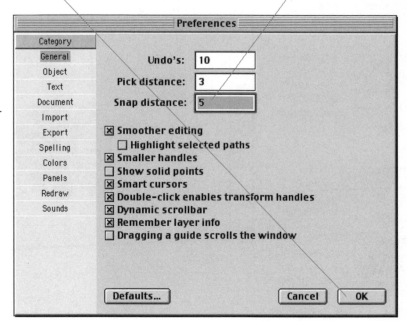

Guides

Guides are similar to the grid in that they are a non-printing aid for positioning. However, unlike the grid, they can be positioned independently on the page. Guides can be placed on a page by dragging them from the ruler or by positioning them precisely with the guides dialog box.

If Snap to Grid is selected, the guides will also snap to the grid when they are positioned.

Dragging guides

The colour of the guides can be changed by selecting Edit> Preferences from the menu bar and then selecting the Colors tab. Click on the Color Palette next to Guide color and select a new colour.

1 Make sure the rulers are showing by selecting View>Page Rulers>Show from the menu bar

2 Click and drag here to place a guide on the page

To make sure guides are visible, select Edit>Guides> Show from the menu bar.

Use the rulers and magnify the page to a sufficient level so that guides can be precisely positioned when dragging.

...cont'd

Guides dialog box

The Guides dialog box contains information about the guides currently on the page and also enables you to add more guides:

The Guides dialog box can also be accessed by double-clicking on a guide that is already on the page.

When adding guides, Count can be used to add a specific number and Increment can be used to enter guides at specified intervals.

If your document has more than one page it is possible to specify the pages on which you want the new guides added. This is done by entering a value in the Page box in the Guides dialog box.

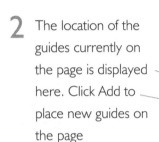

Once the attributes have been set in the Add Guides dialog box and Add has been selected, OK has to then be selected in the Guides dialog box in order for these changes to be applied.

1 Select View>Guides>Edit from the menu bar

2 The location of the guides currently on the page is displayed here. Click Add to place new guides on the page

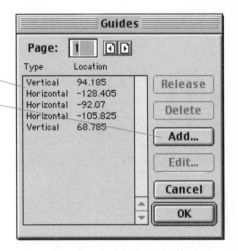

3 Select whether you want to add horizontal or vertical guides

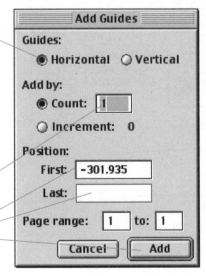

4 Enter the number of guides to be added and the starting and finishing point for them. Select Add

Magnification

When using a drawing program such as Freehand, it is essential to be able to view your work at different magnifications. On occasions you will want to view your entire project on one screen, while on others you will want to zoom in on a particular item within a drawing, for precision editing or manipulation. There are several way to change the magnification of a document:

Menu bar

When creating artwork in Freehand, the magnification should be changed frequently, depending on the type of work that is being undertaken.

Select View>
Magnification from
the menu bar and
then select the
required level of
magnification

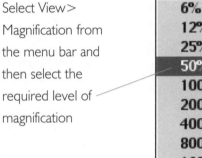

Tools Panel

To decrease magnification with the Zoom tool, hold down Alt when clicking on a page.

Select the Zoom
tool on the Tools
Panel and click on a
page to magnify it

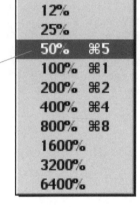

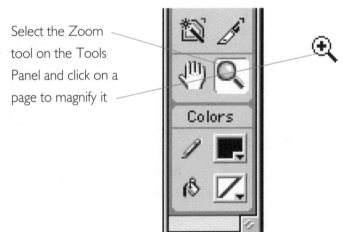

Custom magnification box

Click here and select
a magnification
option

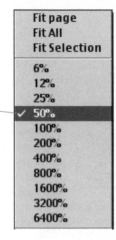

 It is possible to edit existing custom views by selecting View>Custom> Edit from the menu bar and selecting a custom view and then selecting the Redefine button.

Setting custom magnification

1 Select View>Custom>New from the menu bar

2 Enter a
name for the
custom
view. This
takes on the
attributes of the currently selected magnification level. Select OK

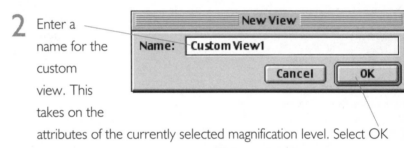

 Custom settings can be created by entering values in the Custom Magnification box, such as 250%. This can then be given a name as a custom view.

3 The new view is
available in the
Custom
Magnification box

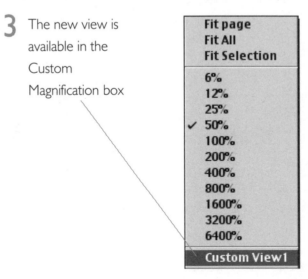

Saving files

For basic file saving, Freehand has the standard Save and Save As commands, which are accessed from the File menu on the menu bar. When files are saved in this way they can be done so in the proprietary Freehand format, which has a '–.fh' file extension, a Freehand template, which has a '–.ft' file extension, or an editable EPS (Encapsulated Postscript) format, whose file extension is '–eps'.

If an EPS file is created it can still be opened again in Freehand and its elements edited independently. However, it will then have to be saved as an EPS file again when the editing is completed.

The Save As command can be used to save a file for the first time, or it can be used to create a copy in another format of a file that has already been saved i.e. create a Freehand template from a file that has already been saved in the standard Freehand format. To use the Save and Save As commands:

When a file is saved in the EPS format it has a small EPS logo next to it in the Open Document dialog box, to identify its type.

| Select File>Save (or Save As) from the menu bar

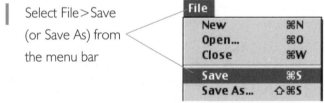

2 Click here to select the required format for the file

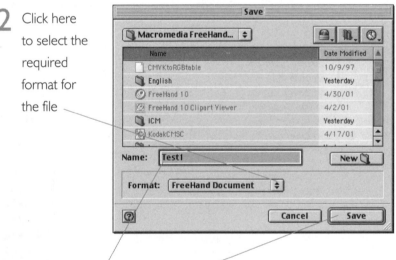

3 Give the file a name and select Save

Exporting files

Since Macromedia recognise that users will want to use their work created in Freehand in a variety of other applications, they have made it possible to export Freehand files into several different formats. These include:

Bitmap images are ones that are made up of physical dots of colour, known as pixels, as opposed to vector graphics.

- Bitmaps, such as GIFs (Graphical Interchange Format), JPEGs (Joint Photographic Experts Group), PNGs (Portable Network Graphic) and TIFFs (Tagged Image Format)

- Various EPS (Encapsulated PostScript) formats

- Enhanced Metafiles

- SWF (Shockwave Flash) format, which is the standard for Flash movies

Only single page documents can be saved in the EPS format.

- Adobe Illustrator

- PICT (Mac only)

- AutoCAD DXF, for use within 3D graphics programs

- PDF (Portable Document Format), for the creation of documents that can be used on a variety of devices using the free Adobe Acrobat reader

PDF is a platform-independent format that is ideal for publishing documents over a variety of devices, while still retaining the original formatting of the document. It is widely used on the web and the free Acrobat reader can be downloaded from the Adobe website at:

www.adobe.com

- RTF (Rich Text Format), for use with popular word processing and desktop publishing programs

Some other file formats are also supported by Freehand and it should be able to export files into a format that can be used by the majority of graphics, web authoring or desktop publishing programs. In general, web authoring programs will use static images in either GIF, JPEG or PNG format and animations in SWF format. For hard copy publishing, TIFF or EPS formats are favoured.

Files can also be exported into formats that are compatible with earlier versions of Freehand and also Illustrator.

Exporting

To export a file:

1 Select File > Export
from the menu bar

The same file can be exported into several different formats. This can be done by selecting Export and saving the file in a different format, or by selecting File>Export Again and then selecting the export format.

2 Click here and select the required export format

For more information on exporting files as Flash movies in the SWF format, see Chapter Nine.

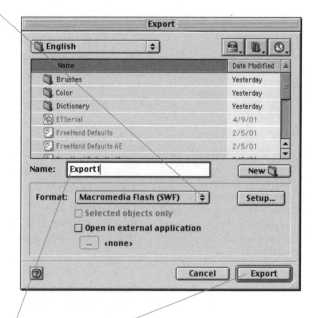

3 Give the file a name and select Export (Mac) or Save (Windows)

Drawing tools

This chapter looks at the drawing tools that are available in Freehand and shows some of the effects that can be created with them.

Covers

Chapter Three

Rectangle tool

As shown in Chapter One, the drawing tools in Freehand are located on the Tools Panel. If this is hidden, it can be made visible by selecting Window>Tools from the menu bar. If a tool has a small triangle in the upper right corner, this means that there is a dialog box associated with the tool, which can be used to edit its attributes. The drawing tools can be used to draw freehand shapes or solid ones such as the Rectangle tool:

1 Double-click here to select the Rectangle tool and to access the Rectangle Tool dialog box

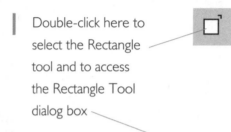

To create a rectangle with right-angled corners, enter a value of 0 (zero) in the Rectangle Tool dialog box.

2 Enter a value here to determine the degree of roundness for the rectangle's corners, or drag this slider. Select OK

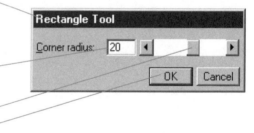

3 Click and drag to create a rectangle. Its corners will have the amount of roundness specified in Step 2

The fill and stroke colours of a rectangle are those that are currently selected at the bottom of the Tools Panel

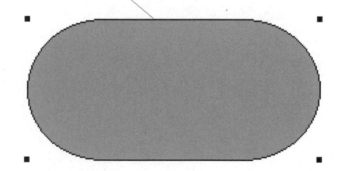

Polygon tool

The Polygon tool can be used to create polygons with varying numbers of sides. To use the Polygon tool:

1 Double-click here to select the Polygon tool and to access the Polygon Tool dialog box

If Star is selected as the required shape, the depth or shallowness of its points can be edited, but not if the Polygon shape option is selected.

2 Enter the number of sides for the polygon and the type of shape required

3 Vary the shape by dragging this slider. Select OK

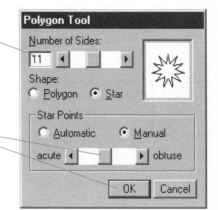

Polygons can be rotated as they are being created on the page. They can also be scaled. However, make sure the mouse button is not released while this is being done. If it is, the Scale and Rotate tools on the Tools Panel will have to be used to perform these same tasks.

4 Click and drag to create a polygon

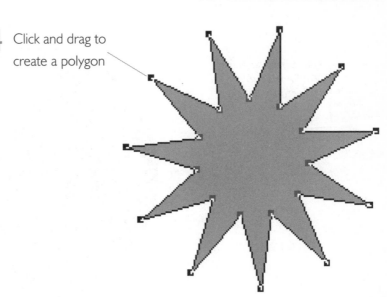

Ellipse tool

The Ellipse tool has no dialog box associated with it.

Drawing ellipses

Select the Ellipse tool and click and drag to create an ellipse

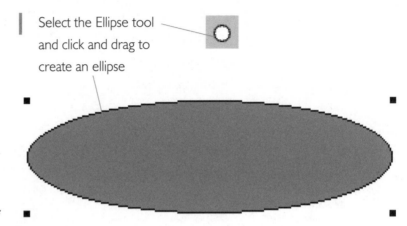

Perfect squares can be created in the same way as circles, by selecting the Rectangle tool and holding down Shift while it is being clicked and dragged on the page.

Drawing circles

Select the Ellipse tool. Hold down Shift and click and drag to create a perfect circle

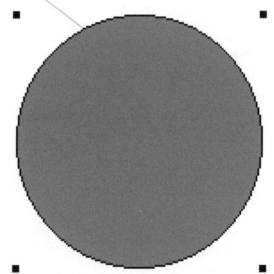

The Stroke and Fill Panels can be used to edit the content of ellipses, and also rectangles and polygons.

Spiral tool

The Spiral tool can be used to create spirals of varying shapes. To use the Spiral tool:

1 Double-click here to select the Spiral tool and to access the Spiral dialog box

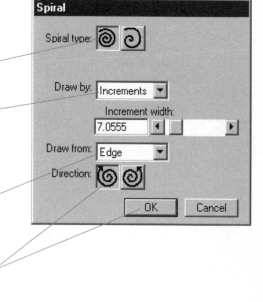

2 Select the type of spiral and the method by which it is drawn

Spirals can either be drawn by Rotations or Increments. If Rotations is selected, a number can be entered to determine how many rotations (or rings of the spiral) are used to create the spiral. If Increments is selected the width between each ring of the spiral can be specified in the dialog box. Then, when the spiral is drawn, new rings are entered as the Spiral tool is dragged, with the incremental value separating each one.

3 Select whether the spiral is drawn from the Center, Edge or Corner and the direction in which it is drawn. Select OK

4 Click and drag to create a spiral

Pen tool

The Pen tool can be used to create irregular shapes out of straight line. It has no dialog box associated with it.

To use the Pen tool:

I Click here to select the Pen tool

The Pen tool can also be used to create curves. To do this, click and hold on the most recently created point and then rotate the tool so that a curve is created.

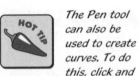

2 Click once on a page to create the first point of an object

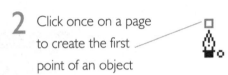

3 Click on another point to create a line between the two

4 Continue in this way to create an irregular shape

For a more detailed look at the Pen tool and how to manipulate objects created with it, see Chapter Four.

Bezigon tool

The Bezigon tool works in a similar way to the Pen tool. One of the differences is that points can be moved immediately after they have been placed. It has no dialog box associated with it.

To finish drawing an object with the Bezigon tool (or the Pen tool) double-click on the last point that has been created. If this is not done, the last point will still be active when you try and create the next shape i.e. the next point that is placed will join with the last point of the original shape.

To use the Bezigon tool:

1 Click here to select the Bezigon tool

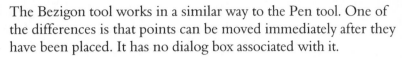

2 Click once on a page to create the first point of an object

3 Click on another point to create a line between the two

Hold down Alt (Windows) or Option (Mac) when placing points to create a curve point rather than the standard corner one.

4 Hold and drag to move points once they have been created

The Bezigon tool can be used to create objects in a variety of ways. For a more detailed look at some of the techniques that can be used, see Chapter Four.

Pencil tool

The Pencil tool can be used to draw genuine freehand objects i.e. the cursor follows the path of your hand as you move the mouse. The Pencil tool has three different options that can be accessed from the Pencil Tool dialog box.

Freehand tools, such as the Pencil tool, in drawing programs, have traditionally been quite jerky and difficult to use. The one here is an improvement on a lot that are currently available, but it still helps if you have a reasonably steady hand when moving the mouse.

To use the Pencil tool:

Freehand style

1 Double-click here to select the Pencil tool and to access the Pencil Tool dialog box

The Precision setting determines how closely the final object resembles the one that you have drawn. If the precision setting is very low (e.g. 1), then the object you draw will have its lines automatically straightened or curved. If the precision setting is high (e.g. 10), the object will be unchanged from your original.

Having a low precision setting can be a good way to iron out any imperfections in a drawing if your technique is a bit jerky.

2 Click here and select the level of precision required. Select OK in the main part of the dialog

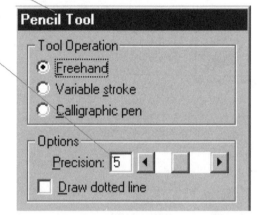

3 Draw a freehand object on the page, working in one continuous movement if possible

Variable Stroke

1 Double-click here to
select the Pencil tool
and to access the Pencil
Tool dialog box

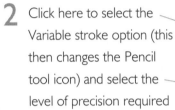

*Check on the
Auto remove
overlap box if
you do not
want any lines
to be visible when
overlapping occurs on the
object.*

2 Click here to select the
Variable stroke option (this
then changes the Pencil
tool icon) and select the
level of precision required

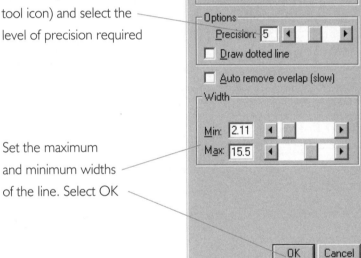

Pencil Tool

Tool Operation
- ○ Freehand
- ⦿ Variable stroke
- ○ Calligraphic pen

Options
Precision: 5
☐ Draw dotted line

☐ Auto remove overlap (slow)

Width
Min: 2.11
Max: 15.5

OK   Cancel

*Make sure your
mouse rollerball
is free of dirt
and as clean as
possible when
using the Pencil tool options.*

3 Set the maximum
and minimum widths
of the line. Select OK

4 Click and drag to
draw a freeform
object that looks like
it has been created
with a paintbrush

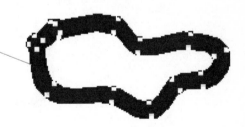

Calligraphic Pen

1 Double-click here to select the Pencil tool and to access the Pencil Tool dialog box

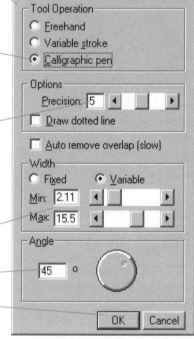

2 Click here to select the Calligraphic pen option (this then changes the Pencil tool icon) and select the level of precision required

Check on the Draw dotted line box to show the object as a dotted line as it is being drawn. The line is still solid when the object is finished, but this makes it quicker for Freehand to create the drawing object.

3 Set the maximum and minimum widths of the line and the angle at which the width of line changes. Select OK

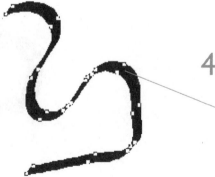

4 Click and drag to draw a freeform object that looks like it has been created with a calligraphic pen

The Calligraphic Pen option can be used to create some interesting text-like effects:

1 Select the options for the Calligraphic Pen

Text that is created with the Calligraphic Pen option is still a drawing object, rather than actual text, in the eyes of the program.

To provide a guide for text created with the Calligraphic Pen, enter some actual text on the page and then trace over it. This will give you a rough idea of the spacing between letters and the alignment of words. For more information about adding text, see Chapter Eight.

2 Draw the outline of the text onto a page

3 Use the color selector on the Tools Panel to add solid colours to the text

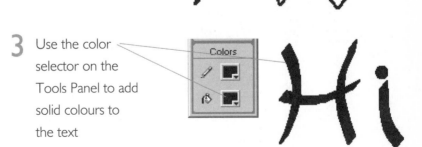

Line tool

The Line tool has no dialog box associated with it. To use it:

1 Select the Line tool and click and drag to create a straight or diagonal line

Lines can be formatted using the Stroke Inspector. If this is not visible, it can be displayed by selecting Window>Inspectors>Stroke from the menu bar.

2 Hold down Alt (Windows) or Option (Mac) to draw the line from the centre, rather than one end. This makes it possible to rotate it as it is being drawn

Paths and points

Paths and points are the foundations on which drawing objects in Freehand are based. This chapter looks at some of the characteristics of paths and points and shows how to edit and manipulate them.

Covers

Chapter Four

Recognising paths and points

Points and paths are the fundamentals of drawing objects in Freehand. They are usually created with the Pen, Bezigon, Line and Freeform tools. However, objects created with the Rectangle, Ellipse, Polygon and Spiral tools are also made up of paths and points.

Paths are continuous lines and they are made up of points that denote the different segments of the path. Paths can be opened or closed and they always have a beginning and an ending point.

Open paths

Open paths are those where the beginning and ending point do not meet. This could be something as simple as a straight line, or a complex shape:

All points have handles that can be used to manipulate them.
Depending on the type of point that is being used, these appear when points are initially inserted or when the path is subsequently selected.

Beginning point   Ending point

Closed paths

Closed paths are those where the beginning and ending points are joined, such as a rectangle or an enclosed shape:

Each path can have up to 32,000 points, but the more points there are, the longer it takes to redraw the picture.

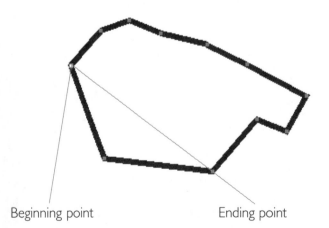

Beginning point   Ending point

Types of points

A new point is inserted whenever there is a new segment of the path i.e. when there is a change in direction. So a straight line would be a path with only two points and a freehand shape could have dozens of points, depending on the complexity of the object. There are different types of points, depending on where they occur within a path. These are corner points, curve points and connector points.

To display the type of point in the Object Inspector, click on it once with the Subselect tool.

Information about points within a path is displayed in the Object Inspector, which can also be used to change the attributes of individual points:

1 To access the Object Inspector, select Window> Inspectors> Object from the menu bar

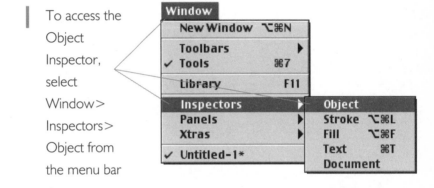

The way in which points are displayed and operate can be edited within the Preferences dialog box. To do this, select Edit>Preferences and select the General tab. Then preferences can be set for the way point handles are displayed, whether points are displayed as hollow or solid and whether they can be edited by double-clicking on them.

2 The type of point is displayed here

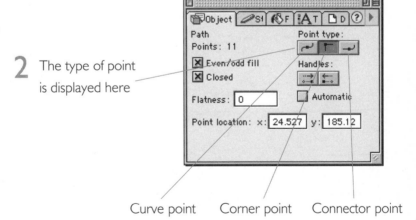

Curve point   Corner point   Connector point

Corner points

Corner points occur either at the beginning of a straight line or whenever two straight lines are joined within a path. This can be created with the Pen, Bezigon, Pencil and Line tools and they can then be edited using the Subselect tool.

To insert and edit corner points:

When a curve point in inserted, the cursor displays a small circle next to it.

1 Click once with one of the drawing tools mentioned above. The best to use in this example are the Pen or Bezigon tool

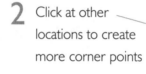

2 Click at other locations to create more corner points

3 Click on the Subselect tool on the Tools Panel and click and drag a corner point to move it

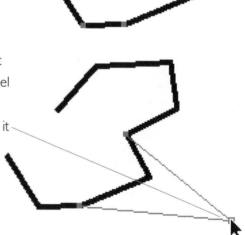

Curve points

Curve points can be placed on a page with either the Pen or the Bezigon tools and then have their shapes edited by dragging their handles.

To insert curve points:

Pen tool

When placing points with the Pen and Bezigon tools, the cursor appear with a small cross next to it, which indicates that it will insert a corner point.

When a curve point is deselected, its transforming handles become hidden.

If a single curve point is placed on a page and then deselected, nothing will be visible. This is because there have to be a minimum of two points to make a curve.

1 Click and drag on a page. The curve point is inserted on the page. This is denoted by a small circle and its transforming handles extend either side

2 Click at another point on the page. A curve will be created between the two points

Bezigon tool

To insert a corner point with the Bezigon tool:

1 Hold down Alt
(Windows) or
Control (Mac) when
you click to insert the
point on the page.
This will insert a
small circle on the
page

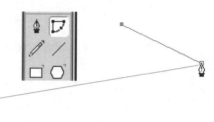

*To finish a
closed path,
double-click on
the beginning
point. To create
an open path, double-click
the ending point or press
the Tab key.*

2 Insert another curve
point on the page

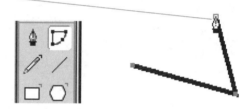

3 Click on the path
between the two
curve points with the
Subselect tool and
drag into the
required position

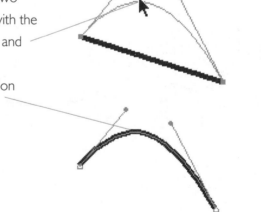

Connector points

To insert a connector point:

1 | Select the Pen tool and hold down Alt and right-click (Windows) or Ctrl+click (Mac). The connector point is denoted by a small triangle

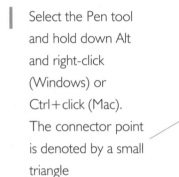

Do not hold down Alt when adding a connector point on a Mac. Just use Ctrl+click.

2 | Add another point and then click and drag between two connector points with the Subselect tool to create a shape with both curved and straight segments

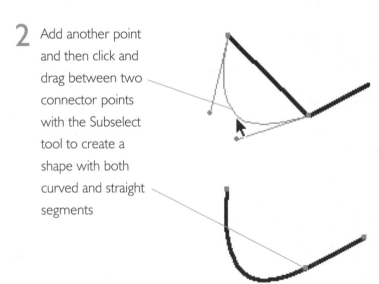

Adding points

It is possible to add numerous points to a path once it has been created. This can enable greater versatility for editing objects. To do this:

Manually

When points are added manually, they are corner points. When they are added using the Xtra Operations toolbar, they are either corner points or curve points, depending on the path to which they are being added.

Select the Pen tool and click to add additional points

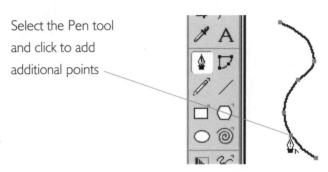

Automatically

Additional points can be added while an existing path is still being created or they can be added to one that has already been created. To do the latter, the path has to first be selected with the Subselect tool.

1 Select a path with the Subselect tool and select Window> Toolbars>Xtra Operations from the menu bar

Each time the Add Points button is clicked, more points are added to the selected path.

2 Click on the Add Point button. This will automatically add points onto the path — halfway between all of the existing points

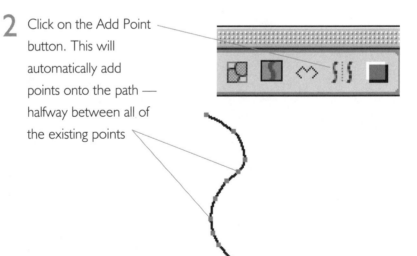

Deleting points and paths

Individual points can be deleted from a path, or whole segments between two points. Also, an entire path can be deleted.

Deleting a path

1 Select the Subselect tool from the menu bar and click once on a path to select it

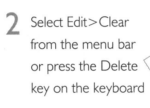

 If the Subselect tool is double-clicked on a path rather than single-clicked this will activate a resizing box around the path. However, the path can still be deleted using the same procedure as in Step 2.

2 Select Edit>Clear from the menu bar or press the Delete key on the keyboard

 The box on the right of the illustrations is only there for comparison purposes.

3 The entire path is removed

Deleting a point

1 Select the Subselect tool from the menu bar and click once on a path to select it

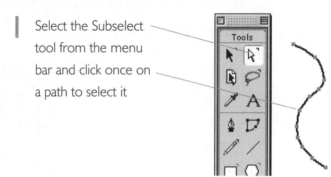

When deleting a point, it can also be selected by clicking on it once with the Pointer tool, once the path has been selected.

2 Click once on a specific point

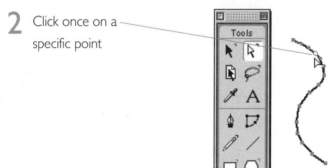

If a point between two corner points is deleted, the subsequent line becomes a straight one between the two corner points. If a point between two curve points is deleted, the subsequent line is a curved one.

3 Press the Delete key on the keyboard. The point is removed and the path segment is adjusted accordingly between the two adjacent points

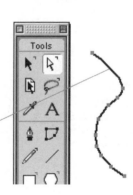

The Pen and Bezigon tools can also be used to delete points. Select one of the tools and position the cursor over the point until a small – sign appears next to it. Click to delete the point.

Deleting a segment

1 Select the Subselect tool from the menu bar and click once on a path to select it. Then click once on a specific path segment

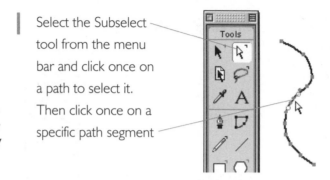

To select multiple segments, hold down Shift and then click on all of the required segments. (Multiple points can also be selected in this way.)

2 Select Edit>Clear from the menu bar or press the Delete key on the keyboard

Edit

Undo Delete	⌘Z
Redo Delete	⌘Y
Cut	⌘X
Copy	⌘C
Copy Special...	
Paste	⌘V
Paste Special...	
Paste In Front	
Paste Behind	
Clear	

Select Edit>Cut in Step 2 to remove a segment from its current location and copy it to the Clipboard. Then, before you copy anything else, select Edit>Paste to paste the segment into a different location. It then takes on the attributes of an independent path.

3 The segment is removed and two separate paths are created, unless the selected segment was at the beginning or end of the path

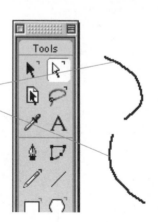

Editing paths

Paths can be reshaped or moved with the Pointer tool and the Subselect tool.

In general, it is safer to move paths by selecting them with the Pointer tool, as individual points and segments could be selected with the Subselect tool by mistake.

Moving paths

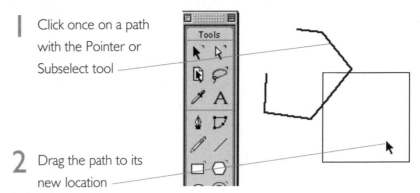

1 Click once on a path with the Pointer or Subselect tool

2 Drag the path to its new location

In addition to editing paths manually, it is also possible to perform some of these tasks with the Object Inspector. If this is not showing, select Window>Inspectors>Object from the menu bar.

Moving points

Individual points can be moved, as well as entire paths:

1 Click once on a path with the Pointer or Subselect tool

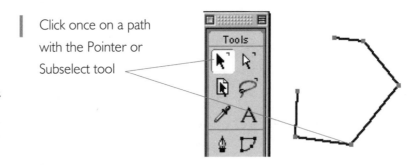

To move more than one point simultaneously, hold down Shift and click on all of the points that you want to move.

A path has to be selected first, before individual points can be selected and moved. If not the whole path will move when you try and move a single point.

2 Click on a point and drag it to its new location.

Moving segments

A segment between two points can also be moved:

1 Click once on a path
with the Subselect tool
to select it

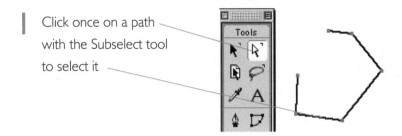

*Paths made up
entirely of
straight lines
do not have an
handles visible
when points are selected.
This is because there are no
curves for the handles to
edit. However, once a curve
is connected to a point, its
handles become visible.*

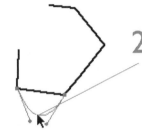

2 Click on a segment
between two points,
and drag to reshape
the segment

Using handles

Some points have handles which can be used to reshape the
segments adjacent to them:

*The way
handles are
displayed can
be determined
by selecting
Edit>Preferences from the
menu bar. Then select the
General tab and check on or
off the Smaller Handles box.*

1 Click once on a path
with the Pointer or
Subselect tool and
click on a point

2 The handles
connected to the
selected point and
also those on either
side are displayed

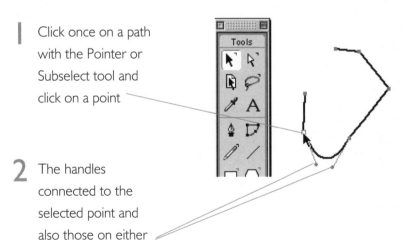

Editing with handles

To decrease the amount of curvature of a curve:

To make a curve bigger, drag the handle away from the point.

Select the end of a handle and drag it towards its point

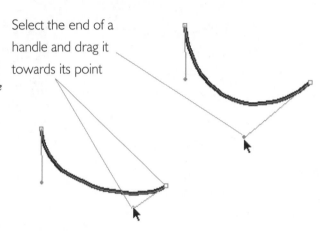

If you drag a segment between two points whose handles are visible, both of the handles will move as the segment is reshaped.

To edit the shape of a curve:

Select the end of a handle and drag it in an opposite direction to the point

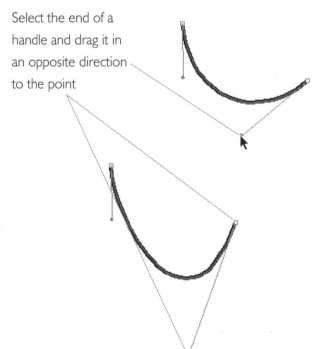

Reshaping paths with handles can be a complex task and it requires a certain amount of practise to perfect it.

Editing with the Freeform tool

The Freeform tool can be used to either 'push' or 'pull' paths into new shapes. This adds an extra dimension for creating objects that have an irregular edge. To reshape objects using the Freeform tool:

Paths that have been pushed and pulled using the Freeform tool can have a more ragged appearance than those that have been created directly with the drawing tools.

The Reshape Area option is similar to the Push/Pull one except that it tapers to a point when it is used. With the Push/Pull option the reshaped area remains at a consistent width, no matter how far it is pushed or pulled.

1 Double-click on the Freeform tool to access the Freeform Tool dialog box

2 Check on the Push/ Pull box and select the required settings. Select OK

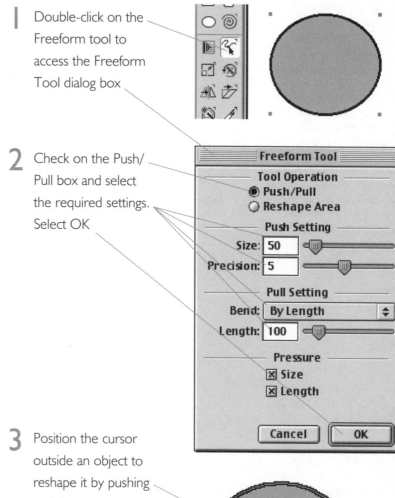

3 Position the cursor outside an object to reshape it by pushing and drag to reshape. (To reshape the object by pulling, place the cursor inside the object and pull outwards)

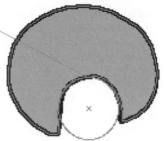

Splitting paths

Paths can be split using the Knife tool. Once this has been done, two separate paths are created. To split a path:

1 Select a path, then double-click the Knife tool on the Tools Panel to access the Knife Tool dialog box

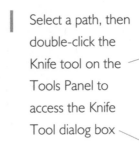

2 Select the required Knife tool options. Select OK

3 Drag the Knife tool across the selected path. This will split the path, creating two new ones that can be edited independently

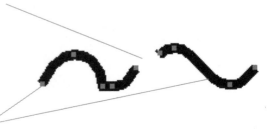

Editing objects

Freehand offers great versatility for editing objects once they have been created. This chapter looks at selecting objects and some of the ways they can be manipulated. It also covers transparency, combining objects, creating blends and tracing objects.

Covers

Chapter Five

Selecting objects

The three tools used to select objects in Freehand are the Pointer tool, the Subselect tool and the Lasso tool. In some cases different tools can be used to perform the same selection task. Before objects are selected with these tools, their options can be set.

Setting tool options

1 Double-click on one of the tools to activate the associated dialog box

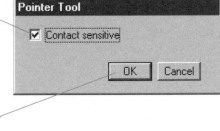

2 Check on the Contact sensitive box if you want to be able to select object that are not entirely enclosed by the selection tool. Select OK

Selecting with the Pointer tool

1 Select the Pointer tool and click once on an object to select it. If it contains no fill, click on the stroke

Selecting with the Subselect tool

Use the Edit>Select option on the menu bar to access a variety of selection options. These are:

- *All*
- *All in Document*
- *None (which deselects all currently selected items)*
- *Invert Selection*

Select the Subselect tool and click once on an object, a path or a point. Only the element that is clicked on is selected

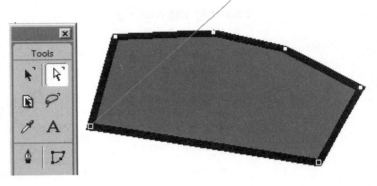

Selecting with the Lasso tool

The Lasso tool is ideal for selecting objects that are irregularly placed i.e. when it is not easy to select them with the Pointer tool.

When making a selection with the Lasso tool, return to the starting point before releasing the drag operation. Otherwise the selection area will not be completed.

Select the Lasso tool and click and drag to select an object. If Contact sensitive is checked off, the whole object has to be enclosed. If it is checked on, the Lasso tool only has to touch the outlines of objects

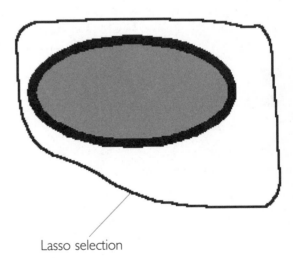

Lasso selection

Scaling

Being able to scale drawing objects is essential in a program such as Freehand and there are a number of ways of doing this. With each method, an object can be scaled in proportion or each axis can be resized independently of the other.

Scaling manually

To deselect an object after it has been selected for scaling, double-click on it again. This should remove the lined box around the object.

Once an object has been selected as in Step 1, it can also be moved by placing the cursor over the object until a four-headed arrow appears. Then click and drag to move the entire object. This does not scale it at all.

To resize an object and retain its original proportions, hold down Shift when the horizontal and vertical axis are being resized together.

1 Select the Pointer tool or the Subselect tool from the Tools Panel and double-click on an object

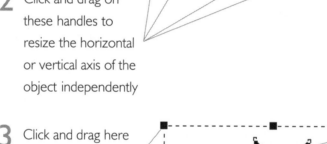

2 Click and drag on these handles to resize the horizontal or vertical axis of the object independently

3 Click and drag here to resize both the horizontal and vertical axis

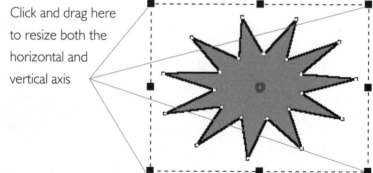

Scaling with the Transform Panel

The Scale option within the Transform Panel can also be accessed by selecting Modify>Transform> Scale from the menu bar.

| Select an object by double-clicking with the Pointer or Subselect tools

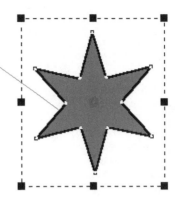

The Transform Panel can also be used to move objects by exact amounts. To do this, select the Move button at the top of the Transform Panel and enter a distance by which you want to move the x– and y–axis of the object. Each time the Move button is clicked in the Transform Panel, the object will be moved by the specified amount.

2 Select Window> Panels> Transform from the menu bar

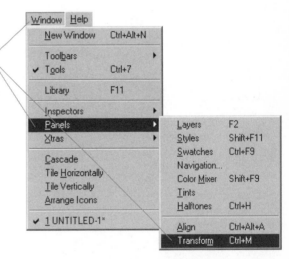

Objects can also be scaled by selecting the Scale tool on the Tools Panel

3 Click on the Scale button in the Transform Panel

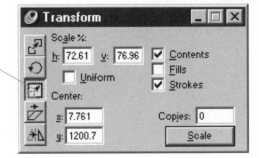

...cont'd

If the Uniform box is checked off and different values are entered for the horizontal and vertical axis, the object will be altered in shape as well as size.

Each time the Scale button is clicked, the selected object is scaled by the specified amount. So if the Scale value is 120% the object will increase by this amount each time the button is clicked.

4 Check on the Uniform box and enter a value here to scale the object to a percentage of its original size

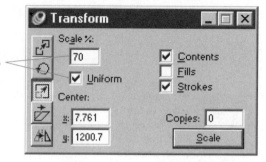

or

Check off the Uniform box and enter percentage values for scaling the horizontal and vertical axis of the object

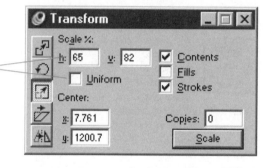

5 Select Scale to apply the changes

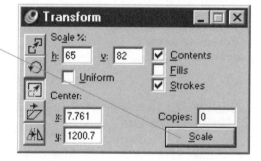

Rotating

Objects can be rotated manually or automatically, in a similar way to scaling them:

Manually

Objects can also be rotated manually using the Rotate tool on the Tools Panel.

1 Double-click on an object with the Pointer or the Subselect tools

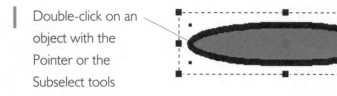

2 Move the cursor outside the object until a curve double-headed arrow appears. Click and drag to rotate the object

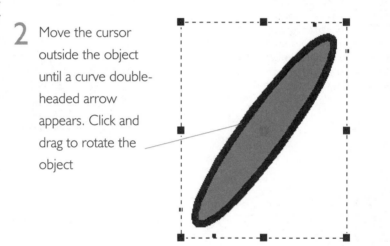

If a value is entered into the Copies box in the Transform Panel, this number of copies of the object will be made and rotated. The original object will remain in the same place and the first copy will be rotated in relation to the original, the second copy will be rotated in relation to the first copy, and so on.

Automatically

1 Select an object and access the Transform dialog box by selecting Window>Panels>Transform from the menu bar

2 Enter the number of degrees here by which you want the object rotated

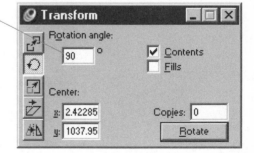

Skewing

The shape of objects can be altered by changing their horizontal or vertical axis, or both. As with scaling and rotating this can be done with the Transform Panel, but an easier way is to use the Skew tool:

1 Select an object with the Pointer or the Subselect tools

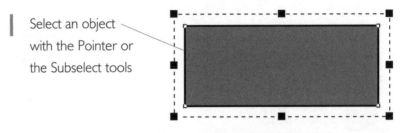

 In the Transform Panel an object can be skewed by entering the amount, in degrees, by which the horizontal and/or vertical axes of the object are to be moved.

2 Select the Skew tool on the Tools Panel and click and drag on a point or segment to skew the object around that point

 If no objects are selected the Transform Panel will be greyed-out i.e. not available, even if it is visible.

3 Click and drag outside the object to skew it and move it simultaneously

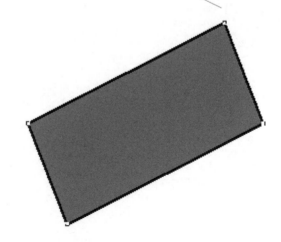

Reflecting

The Reflect tool can be used to create an object as its mirror image. To do this:

1 Select an object with the Pointer or the Subselect tools

2 Select the Reflect tool on the Tools Panel and click on a point around which the mirror image will be created

Reflect tool

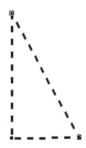

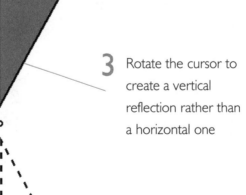

3 Rotate the cursor to create a vertical reflection rather than a horizontal one

Aligning

If a graphic contains items that have to be lined up exactly, you do not have to worry about doing this while they are being created. The different objects can be created and then aligned when they are all completed. Objects can be aligned either vertically or horizontally. To align two or more objects:

| Select the objects to be aligned

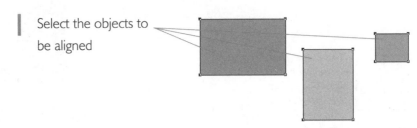

Numerous objects can be aligned at the same time, but a minimum of two objects have to be selected for the Align command to work.

2 Select Modify>Align and then the required alignment option from the menu bar

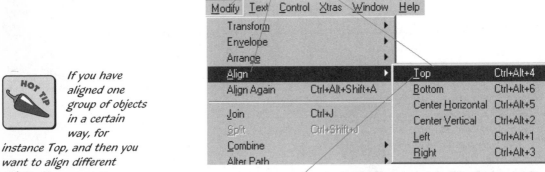

If you have aligned one group of objects in a certain way, for instance Top, and then you want to align different objects the same way, you can select Modify>Align Again from the menu bar and this saves one step of having to select the required alignment option. However, this should only be used if you are sure you want to use the same alignment option as previously.

3 The selected alignment option is applied to the objects

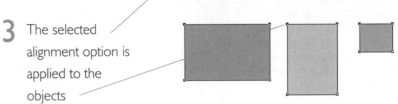

Arranging

If two or more objects overlap on a page it is useful to be able to change their stacking order. This means you can determine which one is on top i.e. completely visible and the order of the subsequent objects. This is done by using the Arrange command:

The options for the Arrange command can place items at any point in the stacking order. The commands are:

- Bring To Front, which moves the object to the top of the stacking order;
- Move Forwards, which moves the selected object forwards one place in the stacking order;
- Move Backward; which moves the selected object back one place in the stacking order;
- Send To Back, which moves the object to the bottom of the stacking order.

Multiple objects can be selected and then arranged together, but it is sometimes easier to arrange objects singly.

1 Select the object to be arranged

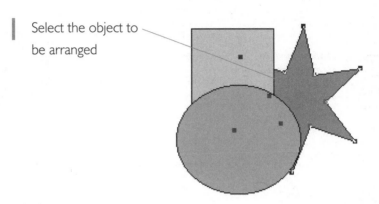

2 Select Modify > Arrange and then the required option from the menu bar

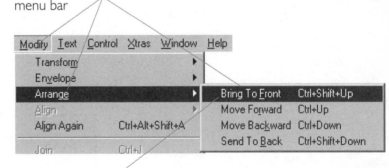

3 The selected Arrange option is applied to the object

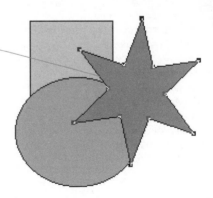

Transparency

Transparency can be applied with objects created in Freehand by defining a new path that gives the appearance of transparency between two or more objects.

To set transparency:

Objects have to have a coloured fill for a transparent effect to be achieved.

1 Select two or more objects that are overlapping

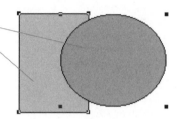

2 Select Modify>Combine>Transparency from the menu bar

A high figure in the Transparency dialog box makes the top object lighter i.e. more transparent, and a low number makes it darker i.e. less transparent.

3 Enter a value in the Transparency dialog box or drag the slider. Select OK

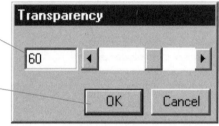

The Transparency dialog box can also be accessed by clicking on the Transparency button on the Xtra Operation toolbar. This is accessed by selecting Window>Toolbars>Xtra Operations from the menu bar. For more information about the Xtra Operations see Chapter Ten.

4 The overlapping area of the objects now appears transparent

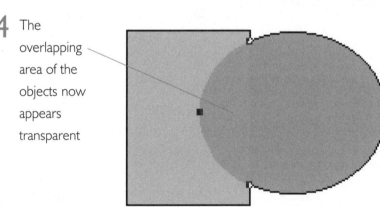

Combining objects

There are several Combine commands that can be used to determine how objects interact with one another. To access the Combine commands:

1 Select two or more objects

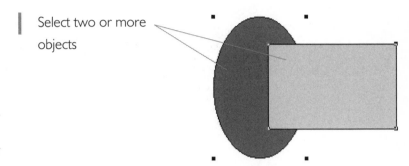

Objects do not have to be overlapping or touching for all of the Union command to be applied to them, but the results are usually more satisfying if they are.

2 Select Modify> Combine from the menu bar and select the required option

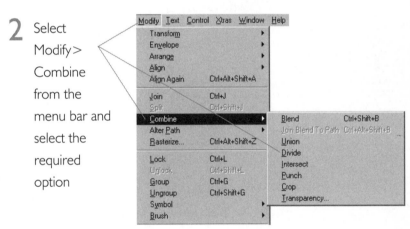

Objects can also be combined by using the Group command. This converts two or more selected objects into a new, single, object. The initial objects do not have to be overlapping or touching for them to be grouped. Objects can be grouped by selecting them and then selecting Modify>Group from the menu bar. Grouped objects can be ungrouped by selecting them and selecting Modify>Ungroup from the menu bar.

Union

This combines two or more objects into a single, composite one:

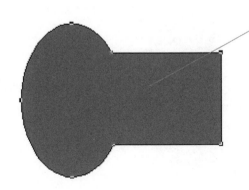

Divide

This breaks apart objects at the point at which they overlap:

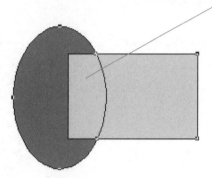

Intersect

This creates a new object out of the area covered by two overlapping objects:

The final Combine command is Crop. This uses the topmost object to trim the objects below it.

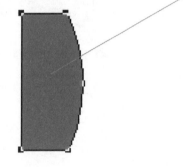

Punch

This removes the topmost object and anything underneath it:

Blending

Blending is a technique that uses two, or more, selected objects and combines them into a single, blended, object by automatically filling in the gaps between them. This is an excellent technique for showing objects such as rectangles and ellipses blending into one another and also for objects of different colours to blend together. To blend two objects together:

Blends can be created between two objects that only have stroke attributes and no fill.

1 Select two objects of different shapes and with different fills

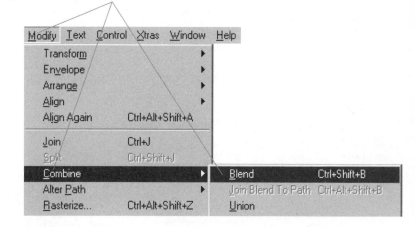

When blends are created, they are done so as a single, grouped object. If it is ungrouped it loses its blend properties.

2 Select Modify>Combine>Blend from the menu bar

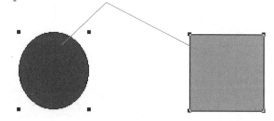

Once a blend object has been created, it can be edited and manipulated in the same way as a standard path.

3 The two objects blend into each other. Both the content and the object shapes are blended

Animated blends can be created and exported into a Flash movie. For more details about this, see Chapter Nine.

Joining blends to paths

After a blend has been created, it is possible to then attach it to a path. This allows for a greater degree of artistic flexibility and it can save a considerable amount of time for certain drawing tasks. To join blends to a path:

The Object Inspector can be used to edit the attributes of a blend once it has been joined to a path. Select Window>Inspectors> Object to access the Object Inspector. The main options are:

- *In the Steps box enter a value for the number of steps used to create the blend from its start to finish. The higher the number of steps, the smoother the blend.*

- *Check on the Show Path box to make the path to which the blend is attached visible.*

- *Check on the Rotate on Path box to change the position of each step of the blend along the path.*

Select Modify> Split to remove a selected blend from its attached path.

1 Create a blend and draw a path to which you want to join it. Select both the blend and the path

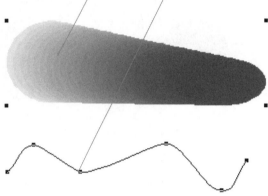

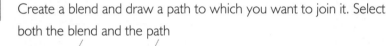

2 Select Modify>Combine>Join Blend to Path from the menu bar

3 The blend now follows the line of the path

Tracing objects

If artwork has been created as a bitmap image, or it has been drawn on paper and then scanned, it is still possible to convert it to a vector path. This is done with the Trace tool:

Bitmap images are those created from pixels, or tiny coloured dots. Vector images are based on a mathematical formula. Traced images convert bitmaps into vectors.

Setting tool options

1 Import a bitmap image. This could be a photograph or a piece of original artwork that has been scanned

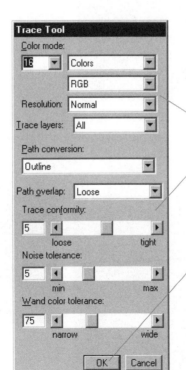

There are several options for determining how the trace tool operates. These include:

- *Color mode, which determines how colours are selected and converted;*
- *Resolution, which affects the quality of the traced image;*
- *Trace layers, which determines which layers are included in the trace;*
- *Path conversion, which determines how paths are created;*
- *Path overlap, which determines how overlapping paths are dealt with;*
- *Wand color tolerance, which determines how pixels of similar colour are traced.*

2 Double-click the Trace tool on the Tools Panel

Trace Tool

Color mode:
18 Colors
RGB
Resolution: Normal
Trace layers: All
Path conversion:
Outline
Path overlap: Loose
Trace conformity:
5 loose   tight
Noise tolerance:
5 min   max
Wand color tolerance:
75 narrow   wide
OK   Cancel

3 Set the required Trace options in the Trace dialog box. Select OK

Traced images can take up more file space than the original bitmap from which they were created.

Specific colours within an object can also be traced. To do this, click on the required colour in the bitmap with the Trace tool. Then double-click on the selected area and select Trace Selection in the Wand Options dialog box. Select OK to trace the selection.

The Magic Wand tool is used to select similar colours. Its tolerance can be set so that it selects a narrow or wide range in relation to the initially selected colour.

Before a traced object is moved, select Modify>Group from the menu bar so that it can easily be moved as a single object. Otherwise the individual paths could be selected and moved instead.

4 Click and drag the Trace tool to select the area to be traced

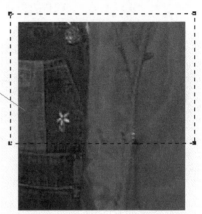

5 The traced area is placed directly on top of the original artwork

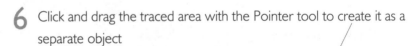

6 Click and drag the traced area with the Pointer tool to create it as a separate object

Editing content

This chapter looks at how colour can be created and added to objects in the form of fills and strokes. It also shows how objects can be manipulated with envelopes and perspective grids.

Covers

Chapter Six

Swatches Panel

The ability to use, edit and create colours in a drawing program is essential and Freehand offers an extensive and sophisticated range of techniques in relation to this. One of the most fundamental is the Swatches Panel which displays the currently available colours for the current document. The Swatches Panel displays important information about the colours within it:

1 Select Window>Panels>Swatches from the menu bar

The colours that are displayed in the Swatches Panel are the same as those that are available in the Color boxes for Fill and Stroke at the bottom of the Tools Panel. If a colour is added to the Swatches Panel, it will also appear in the swatches for these boxes.

2 Select a colour to display its colour information

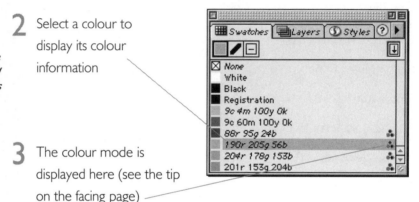

3 The colour mode is displayed here (see the tip on the facing page)

The buttons at the top left of the Swatches Panel can be used to specify colours for the fill and stroke of an object. Click on one of the buttons and then select a colour for this to be applied to that part of an object.

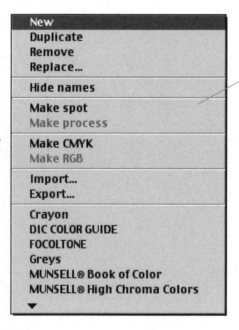

4 Click ▶ in the Panel to access the Swatches Panel menu

Color Mixer Panel

The Color Mixer Panel allows you to create you own colours, using a variety of methods, depending on the selected colour system:

1 Select Window>Panels>Color Mixer from the menu bar to display the Color Mixer Panel

Colours in the Color Mixer Panel can be created using four different methods. These are denoted by the four buttons down the left-hand side of the Color Mixer Panel and they are:

- *CMYK mode. This creates colours using different quantities of Cyan, Magenta, Yellow and Black;*

- *RGB mode. This creates colours using different quantities of Red, Green and Blue;*

- *HLS mode. This creates colours using different values of Hue, Lightness and Saturation;*

- *System Color mode. This creates colours according to the system colours provided by your computer's operating system. These differ for PC and Mac.*

2 Select one of these buttons for a particular colour system

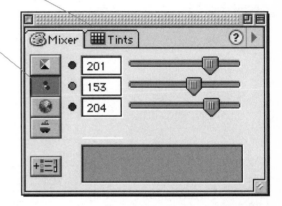

3 Create custom colours by dragging these sliders

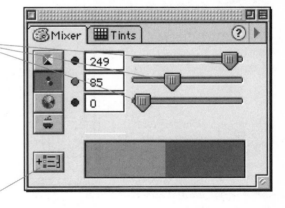

4 Click here to add a custom colour to the Swatches Panel

Tints Panel

The Tints Panel allows you to create colours that are based on a solid colour but which are a lighter version, or tint, of the base colour.

To use the Tints Panel:

There is also a Halftones Panel, but this is concerned with the printing process, rather than adding colours to documents.

1 Select Window>Panels>Tints from the menu bar to display the Tints Panel

3 Select a percentage amount for the tint colour (as a proportion of the base colour) or drag this slider

2 Click here and select a colour from the Swatches Panel drop-down list on which to base the tint colour.

The default colour in the Tints Panel is the same as the currently selected one in the Mixer Panel.

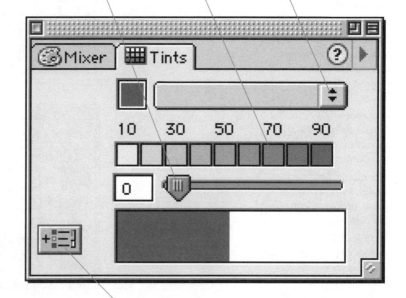

Tints of a base colour are an excellent option if you want to display a lot of subtle variations of a colour. For instance, if you are drawing a forest, or depicting skin tones.

4 Click here to add the new colour to the Swatches Panel

Adding colours

Colours can be added from the Swatches, Color Mixer and Tints Panels:

Swatches Panel

Pantone is the design industry standard for colour definition. If you are using a commercial printer for the output of Freehand documents they may ask for a list of the Pantone colours that have been used, to make it easier for them to create them in the printed version.

If your graphic is going to be used on the web, you can select a library of web-safe colours from the Swatches Panel menu. This will ensure that the colours that are used will be the ones that are seen when the graphic is viewed through a browser.

This is necessary because browsers are only guaranteed to display a certain number of colours (approximately 256) in exactly their correct format. However, if a web-safe palette is used, this should not be an issue.

1 Click here to access the Swatches Panel menu and select one of the available colour libraries

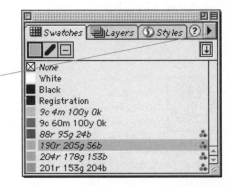

2 Select a colour from the library swatch and select OK

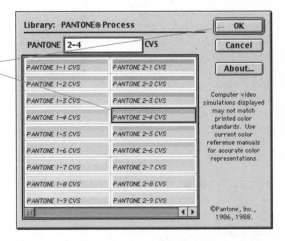

3 The colour is added to the Swatches Panel, using its library name and attributes

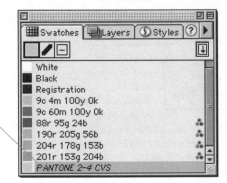

Colours created in the Tints Panel are displayed as a percentage value of the base colour when shown in the Add to Swatches dialog box.

In the Add to Swatches dialog box, there is an option for specifying colours as Process or Spot. These refer to how the colours will be printed. Process colours are created by combining CMYK (Cyan, Magenta, Yellow and Black inks) while spot colours use special premixed inks.

If you are in any doubt about which method to use, consult your printer. This is not an issue if your graphics are only going to be displayed electronically.

When a new colour is added to the Swatches Panel, its attributes and colour mode are displayed.

Colours can also be added to the Swatches Panel by dragging them there from the colour box of either the Color Mixer or Tints Panel.

Color Mixer and Tints Panels

1 Create a colour using the right method for each Panel

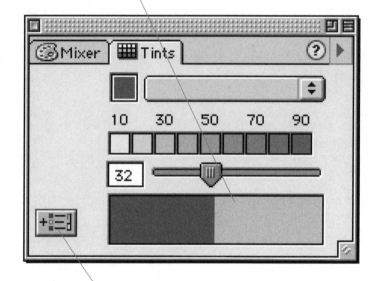

2 Click on this button

3 In the Add to Swatches dialog box, the colour information is displayed here. Select Add to add the colour to the Swatches Panel

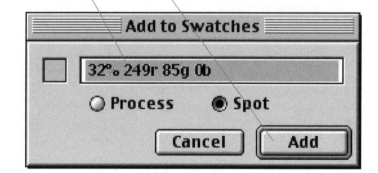

Editing colours

Naming colours

Naming colours is important because if you are using a lot within the same document is can be easy to become confused, particularly if you are using a lot of tints or similar colours.

1 Double-click on a colour in the Swatches Panel

2 Overtype with a new name

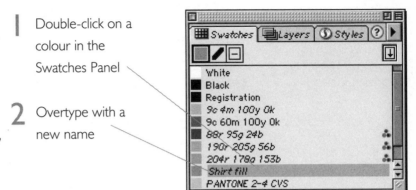

Deleting colours

1 Select a colour in the Swatches Panel and click here to select the menu. Select Remove

The Swatches Panel menu can also be accessed by right-clicking (Windows) or Ctrl+clicking (Mac) on a colour and then selecting the required command.

2 If the colour is being used in the document a warning dialog box will appear. Select Remove

Xtras colour options

The Xtras menu offers a number of options for editing colours and altering the way they are displayed in the Swatches Panel.

To access the Xtras options:

1 Select Xtras>Colors from the menu bar

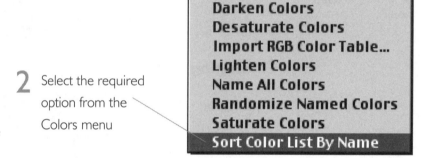

Color Control...
Convert to Grayscale
Darken Colors
Desaturate Colors
Import RGB Color Table...
Lighten Colors
Name All Colors
Randomize Named Colors
Saturate Colors
Sort Color List By Name

Some editing functions can be performed within the Stroke and Fill Inspectors and these are looked at in the rest of this chapter.

2 Select the required option from the Colors menu

3 Any option that is selected (here, Sort Color List by Name) is applied in the Swatches Panel

Swatches | Layers | Styles

None
White
Black
Registration
9c 60m 100y 0k
Apricot
Light Green
Orange
PANTONE 2-4 CVS
Pink

Applying colours

Colours can be applied to objects using the Stroke and Fill Inspectors, and this is looked at in the rest of the chapter. However, there are some techniques whereby colours can be applied by using the Swatches, Color Mixer and Tints Panels:

Swatches Panel

In the Swatches Panel, the Fill Color button is the one on the left and the Stroke button is the one to the right of it.

1 Select an object and access the Swatches Panel

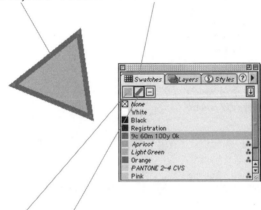

2 Select the fill and stroke buttons and select the required colour

Color Mixer and Tints Panels

If a colour is dragged from the Color Mixer or Tints Panels onto an object, this colour will be added to the object (but only if it has previously been added to the Swatches Panel).

1 Select an object and access the Color Mixer or Tints Panels

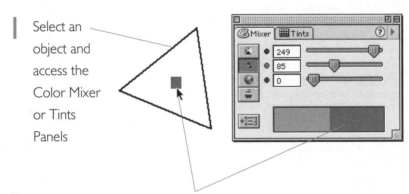

2 Click on a colour and drag it to either the stroke or the fill of the object

Fill Inspector

The Fill Inspector is used to specify the fill for a selected object. It offers considerable variety in terms of colours and patterns. The basic fill is a solid colour, but there are several other options for the fill of an object. To add a basic fill:

The colour displayed in the Fill Inspector changes according to the selected object in the document and its fill colour.

I   Select an object (it does not matter what fill it currently has)

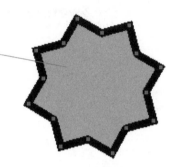

2   Select Window>Inspectors>Fill to access the Fill Inspector

If two or more objects with different fills are selected simultaneously, the Fill Inspector will be blank initially. However, it is then possible to select a fill colour that will be applied to all of the selected objects, regardless of their original fills.

3   Click here to select a solid colour for the new fill for the object. This will be a list of the currently available colours in the Swatches Panel and is just another way to add a solid colour to an object

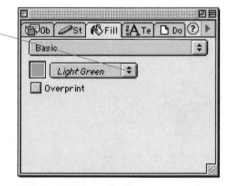

Changing fills

The Fill Inspector has a wide variety of options for applying fills to objects. To access them:

Click here on the Fill Inspector and select an option from the drop-down menu

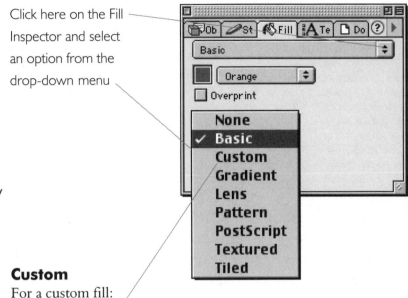

Each custom fill has its own options, that can be edited to change the appearance of the fill.

Custom

For a custom fill:

Custom fills are only visible when printed on a PostScript printer.

Select Custom and click here for the Custom options

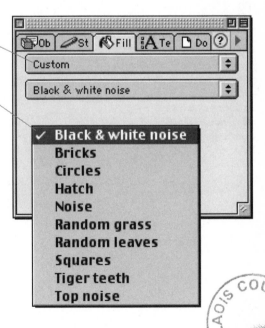

Gradient

Gradient fills are one of the most versatile effects available in Freehand. To create them:

Gradients are excellent for creating textured effects in pictures and also for conveying a sense of light e.g. a gradient could be used to simulate the effect of light shining on a particular part of an object. Several different objects, each with their own gradient fills, can also be combined for dramatic effects.

1 Click here in the Fill Panel and select Gradient

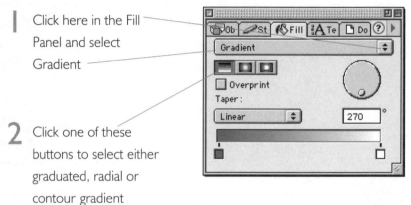

2 Click one of these buttons to select either graduated, radial or contour gradient

A graduated gradient creates an effect that fades out from top to bottom or vice versa; a radial gradient creates a circular gradient, from a centre point; and a contour gradient creates a rectangular gradient from a centre point.

3 For a radial or contour gradient, drag this marker to change the centre point of the gradient

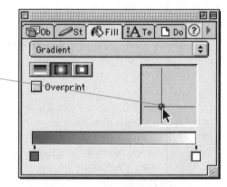

or

For a graduated gradient, drag this dial to change the degree at which the gradient appears

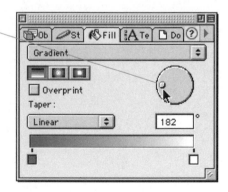

4 Click and drag a gradient marker to add a new one to the gradient

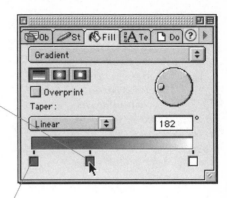

The greater the number of colours that are added to a gradient, the more noticeable the effect is and the gradient can look like a group of rings rather than a smooth transition from one colour to another. For the subtlest gradient use only two colours.

5 Click once on a gradient colour marker and select a new colour for it from the Swatches Panel

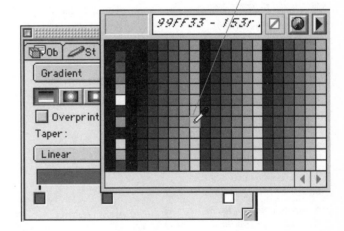

Drag the colour markers in the Gradient dialog box to move the position of that colour within the gradient.

When you are creating or editing a gradient, make sure the object to which it will be applied is visible, so that you can view the effect of the changes as they are being made.

Graduated gradient   Radial gradient   Contour gradient

Check on the Snapshot box in the Lens fill dialog box to enable the lens effect to be moved anywhere on the page while the original object below remains intact.

The options for the lens fill determine the appearance of any objects underneath it. They are:

- *Transparency, which creates a level of transparency which can be specified in the Opacity box.*
- *Magnify, which increases the size of the object below, as if it were being viewed through a magnifying glass;*
- *Invert, which reverses the colour of the object below;*
- *Lighten, which lightens the colour of the object below to a specified amount;*
- *Darken, which darkens the colour of the selected object to a specified amount;*
- *Monochrome, which displays the object below as a black and white tint of the selected colour.*

Lens

Lens fills create a special effect for the selected object, which impacts on any objects below it.

To create a lens fill:

1 Click here in the Fill Panel and select Lens

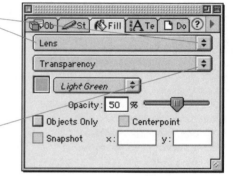

2 Click here to select an option for the lens

3 Select options for the selected type of lens

4 Any object with a lens fill impacts on any objects below it. In this example the selected object has a Transparency lens fill, allowing the object below to be visible

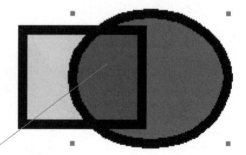

Pattern

Pattern fills consist of predefined patterns that can be applied to objects:

There are 64 predefined patterns in the Fill Panel. The colour of these can be changed in the Panel once they have been selected.

1 Click here in the Fill Panel and select Pattern

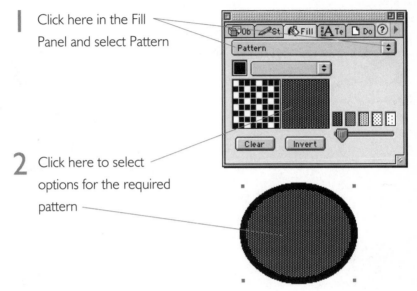

2 Click here to select options for the required pattern

PostScript and Textured fills are fills that do not appear in the Freehand document, but are visible when they are printed on a PostScript printer. Textured fills can be applied in a similar way to Pattern fills.

Tiled

This can be used to create a tiled fill using an existing object:

1 Copy an existing object and select the Tiled option in the Fill Panel

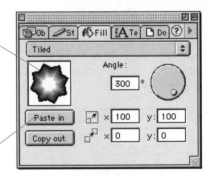

2 Select another object and select Paste in to create a tiled fill with the object copied above

Stroke Inspector

The Stroke Inspector is used to specify the stroke for a selected object.

To specify a basic stroke:

If a setting of None is selected for the stroke of an object, the stroke will be completely transparent.

1 Select an object or create a new path

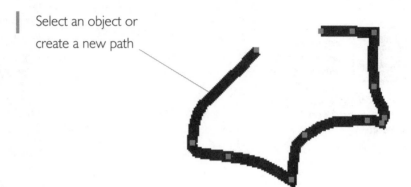

2 Select Window>Inspectors>Stroke to access the Stroke Inspector

If the stroke attributes are selected in the Stroke Inspector when no object is selected in a document, this will become the default stroke until another one is specified. However, if an object is selected, the new stroke style will only apply to that object. This also applies to the Fill Panel.

Click here to select a stroke colour

Click here to select a cap style (this is the appearance of the end of a stroke)

Click here to specify how two strokes join together

Click here to select arrowhead styles

Click here to select a dashed line

Click here to select a stroke width

Changing strokes

Various stroke styles can be selected, in a similar way to those used in the Fill Panel.

Custom

Select Custom and click here for the Custom options

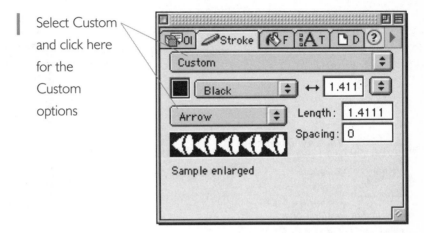

The PostScript stroke option is for use when your document is going to be output to a PostScript printer.

Pattern

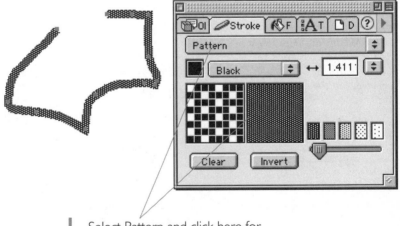

Select Pattern and click here for the Pattern options

Graphic envelopes

Freehand envelopes can be used to distort objects by placing them within a confined space. The object then has to redraw itself within the space. This is a useful device for creating unusual shapes while still retaining the whole view of an object. To create envelopes for graphics:

1 Select an object

The drop-down list on the Envelope toolbar contains a list of available envelope styles. Select one of these and then click on the button to the left of the menu to apply the envelope to a selected object.

To create your own preset envelope, select an envelope that you have created and select Modify>Envelope>Save As Preset. This will then be added to the list of available envelopes in the drop-down list.

2 Select Window> Toolbars>Envelope from the menu bar

3 Select a style for the

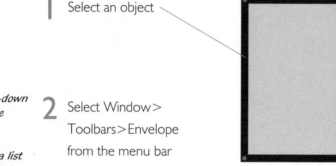

envelope and click on the Create button on the Envelope toolbar

4 The object is placed in the appropriate style of envelope. Manipulate the envelope to see how the object reacts

Adding perspective

Perspective grids are non-printing items, which means they do not appear in the published document, either in hard copy or on the web.

Perspective is a powerful drawing device and Freehand has a grid that can be used to add a sense of perspective to objects. To create a perspective grid and add objects to it:

1 Select View>Perspective Grid>Define Grids from the menu bar

The main element of a perspective grid is its vanishing point. There are three options for this:

- *A value of 1 creates a shape like a single wall, with its vanishing point at the far end*

- *A value of 2 creates a shape like two walls moving away from each other in a V shape, with a vanishing point at the far end of each of them.*

- *A value of 3 creates a shape like a pyramid, with a vanishing point at each corner and at the top.*

2 Enter the settings for the grid and select OK

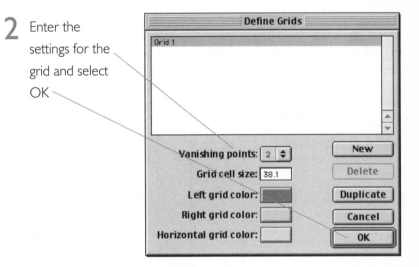

3 Select View> Perspective Grid>Show from the menu bar. The Perspective Grid will be placed over any content that is already on the page

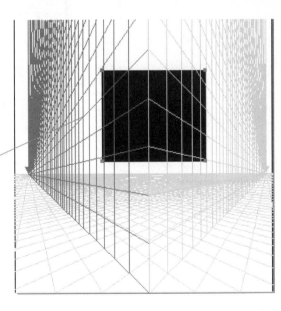

The Define Grids dialog box can be used to create and name several perspective grids with different attributes. This can be used to give different objects a different sense of perspective within the same document.

...cont'd

4 Select the Perspective tool from the Tools Panel

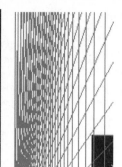

If an object is dragged onto a perspective grid without the Perspective tool first being selected, nothing will happen to the object and it will not be applied to the grid. This is true also for objects that are created directly onto a perspective grid.

5 Click and drag the required object and place it within the perspective grid. Do not release the mouse button

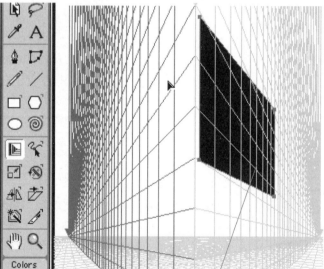

For a perspective grid that only has one vanishing point, the Up or Down arrow keys place the object on the horizontal grid and the Left or Right keys place it on the vertical grid. A perspective grid has to have a minimum of two vanishing points for it to be possible to attach an object to the floor of a grid.

6 Click the Up or Down arrows on the keyboard to place the object on the floor of the perspective grid, or select the Left or Right arrow to place it on the wall

Improving workflow

This chapter looks at some of the techniques for making the editing process more efficient. These include the use of layers for ordering workflow, symbols for creating reusable items and styles for consistent formatting effects.

Covers

Chapter Seven

Layers Panel

In complex graphics it is useful to be able to place different elements of an illustration on different layers within the same document. This is similar to drawing different items on plates of glass and then layering them together to see the final, complete image. One of the advantages of this is that specific elements of an image can be edited independently from one another and it gives more control over the creative process. In Freehand this technique is controlled by the Layers Panel, which enables new layers to be added and existing ones manipulated so that the authoring process can be as efficient as possible.

Using layers can be thought of in the same way as stacking objects on top of each other. However, objects on different layers cannot interact with one another.

To access the Layers Panel:

Non-printing layers, such as the background layer, can be used as a guide for the final graphic. Objects can be created over a draft image that resides on the background layer. This is particularly useful if draft artwork has been produced, from which is required a final Freehand illustration.

Select Window> Panels> Layers from the menu bar

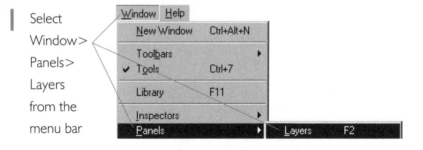

To change a non-printing layer into a printing one, or vice versa, drag it over the separator line.

A document's layers are shown here. Items above the separator bar are printable items and items below it are non-printing

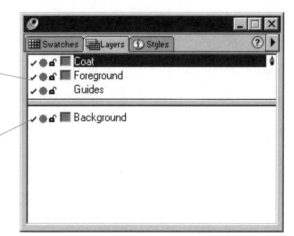

Adding layers

In general, it is good practice to include any new element in a graphic on a new layer. This makes it easy to work with, knowing that it will not get mixed up with items on other layers. To add layers to a document:

1 Click here on the Layers Panel and select New

The topmost layer in the Layers Panel is the one that appears at the top of the stacking order in the document i.e. it will cover any objects on layers below it.

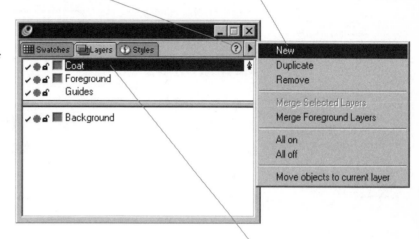

Layers can be deleted by selecting Remove from the Layers menu. However, this removes all of the content of that layer as well, so double-check when you are deleting layers.

2 The name of the new layer will be highlighted. Double-click it and overtype it to give it a unique name

3 When content is added, it will be placed on the selected layer in the Layers Panel

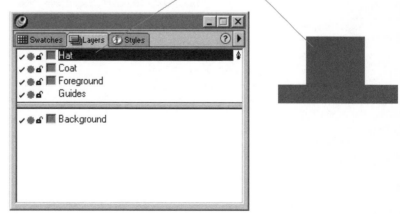

Working with layers

Selecting layers

To select all the objects on a layer, hold down Alt (Windows) or Option (Mac) when the layer name is selected in the Layers Panel.

Click on a layer in the Layers Panel to select it. Any content that is added will be placed on this layer

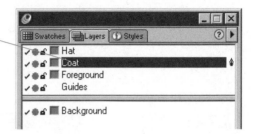

Moving layers

Always view the results carefully when you move layers, to make sure that the change in stacking order has not adversely changed the appearance of the image.

Click and drag a layer to move it in the Layers Panel. This will change the stacking order of any items on that layer

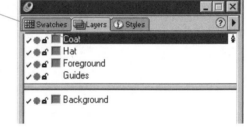

Moving Objects

To move objects in a document between layers:

To make sure you can move objects between layers in this way, check that Clicking on a Layer Name Moves Selected Objects is checked on in the Panels tab of the Preferences dialog box.

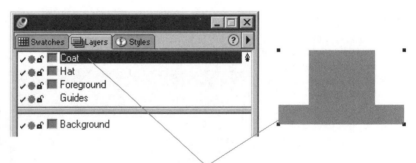

Select an object and select a new layer in the Layers Panel to move it to that layer

Hiding layers

It can be useful to hide layers, and their contents, so that the document window looks less cluttered while you are working on other elements.

To do this:

When a layer has been hidden, its content is still there, it is just not visible. This is not the same as deleting a layer, which results in all of the layer's content being removed.

Click here to hide a layer and its contents

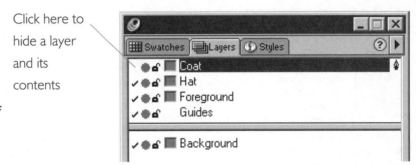

When a layer is locked, this is denoted by the padlock icon next to it becoming closed rather than open.

Locking layers

If you have added important content to a particular layer and you do not want it to be accidentally altered, this can be achieved by locking the layer. This means that it cannot be edited until it is unlocked.

To do this:

To make layers visible again and also unlock them, click at the same point as for hiding and locking them respectively.

Click here to lock a layer and its contents

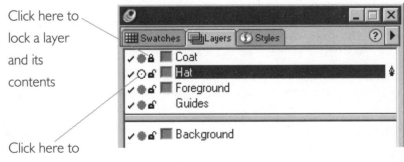

When a graphic has been completed, it is possible to merge layers in order to make the final file smaller in size. To do this, select the layers you want to merge by Shift+clicking on them in the Layers Panel. Then select Merge Selected Layers from the Layers Panel menu.

Click here to view an unlocked layer's content in outline

Library Panel

The Library is the storage area in Freehand where the frequently used items are contained. Items that are stored in the Library are known as symbols. They can then be inserted into a document, at which point they become known as instances.

Accessing the Library

1 If the Library is not already showing, select Window>Library from the menu bar

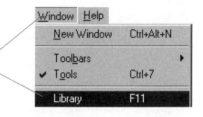

2 Select an item and it will be displayed in the Preview window. The items in the Library are displayed here

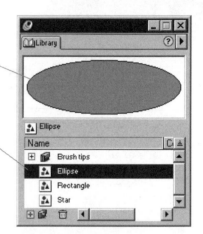

3 Click here to rearrange the items in the Library

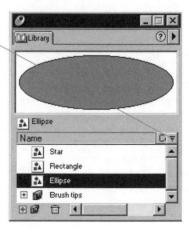

Creating symbols

Any object, group or text can be converted into a symbol, at which point it is automatically added to the Library.

Newly created symbols have the default name Graphic and then the next available sequential number. To give a symbol a unique name, double-click on it and overtype with a new name.

Drag a selected object into this portion of the Library

or

Select an object and select Modify > Symbol > Convert to Symbol from the menu bar

or

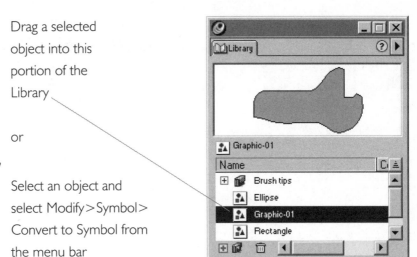

A selected object can also be converted into a symbol by clicking here on the Library Panel and selecting New Graphic from the menu.

To edit a symbol in the Library, double-click on its icon and then make the changes in the symbol editing environment. These changes will apply to any instances of the symbol that have already been created.

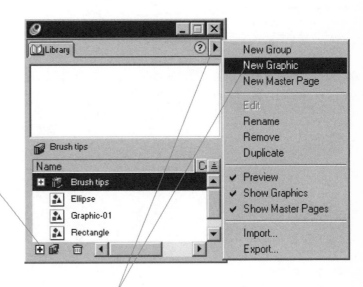

Select an object and click here on the Library Panel

Working with instances

Creating instances

Instances can be created in a document from any symbol in the Library. To do this:

Once instances have been created, they can be edited and manipulated, without altering the original symbol.

Drag a symbol from here onto a page in a document

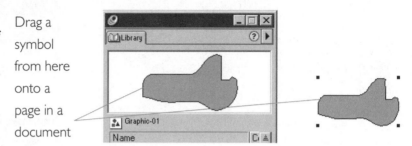

Releasing instances

Instances can be released so that they do not refer back to their original symbol. This means that any editing changes that are applied to the symbol will not now affect the object since it is no longer an instance. To release an instance:

If a symbol is deleted from the Library, all instances of it can be removed from the document. However, before this is done, a warning dialog box appears, asking if you want to release all the instances of the symbol and convert them to ordinary objects or delete them. Select an option accordingly.

1 Select an instance

In Freehand, a symbol is known as a parent and any instance created from it is known as a child.

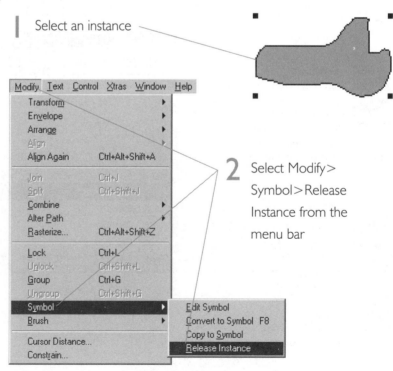

2 Select Modify> Symbol>Release Instance from the menu bar

Exporting symbols

If you have created a symbol that you want to use in another document, you can export is so that it is available elsewhere within Freehand. To do this:

1   Click here to access the Library menu and select Export

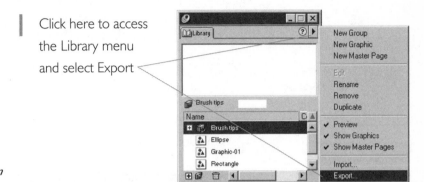

To select more than one symbol to be exported at a time, hold down Shift and then click on all of the symbols to be exported in the Export Symbols dialog box.

2   Select a symbol to export and select Export

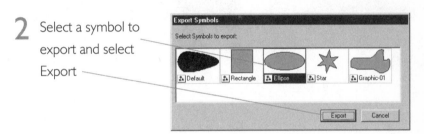

3   Browse to the location where you want to store the symbol. Enter a name for the exported symbol and select Save

To import a symbol into a new document, select Import from the Library menu and browse to where the symbol has previously been exported to. Select it and select Open then select it in the Import Symbol dialog box and select Import to add it to the Library of the new document.

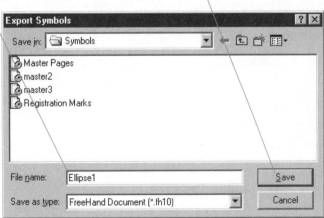

Styles Panel

Styles can be created for both text and graphical objects. This is a set of formatting instructions that can be applied to text or objects and it is an excellent device for maintaining consistency of design and also formatting a lot of objects quickly. Styles are created in the Styles Panel and then they can be applied to objects and text within the active document. To display the Styles Panel:

Styles in Freehand are similar to those used for formatting text in word processing or desktop publishing programs. The main difference is that styles can also be created for objects in Freehand.

In Styles name mode, the styles are displayed by their name and a letter A or a square for text and object styles respectively.

1 Select Window>Panels>Styles from the menu bar

2 Click here. In the menu, select Show Names to display the styles with their names only

3 Click here and select Hide Names to display a preview of the available styles

Creating styles

Styles can be created by either selecting an object or block of text and adding its format to the Styles Panel, or by copying an existing style and then editing it.

The styles in the Styles Panel are known as the parent styles. When a style is applied to an object or a block of text, it is known as a child style.

Creating styles from existing items

To create a new style from an existing one, select the style and select New from the Styles menu to create a new style or Duplicate to create a copy of the existing one. In both cases the new style can be renamed and edited to give it its own unique attributes (see the next page for details about editing styles).

1 Select an object or block of text in a document

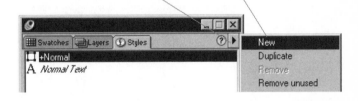

2 Access the Styles Panel. Click here and select New from the menu

Styles can be renamed by double-clicking on them in the Styles Panel and then overtyping with a new name. To do this, the Styles Panel has to be in the Show Name mode.

3 The attributes of the selected object or text will be added to the Styles Panel as a new style

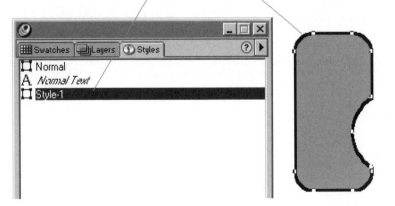

Editing styles

Select a style. Click here to access the Styles menu and select Edit

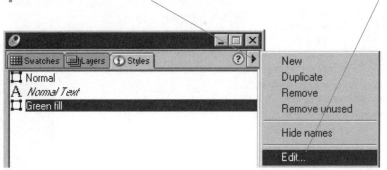

If a text style is being edited the available options will be for text formatting rather than object formatting. For more information on creating and formatting text, see Chapter Eight.

2 Enter the attributes for the new style

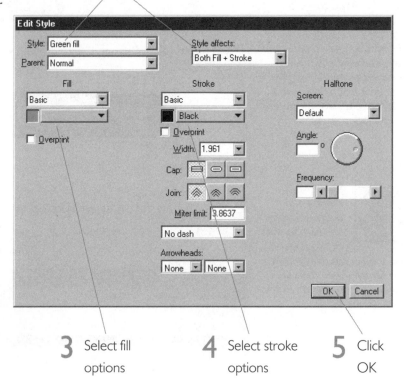

If a style is edited in the Styles Panel (the parent style) all of the objects or text which have had that style applied to them (child styles) will be updated with the new style.

3 Select fill options

4 Select stroke options

5 Click OK

Applying styles

Styles can be applied by selecting them from the Styles Panel or dragging and dropping them onto objects.

Selecting from the Styles Panel

1 Select an object or text block

When applying styles it is better to have the Styles Panel showing in preview mode. This allows you to see exactly how the style will be displayed.

2 Click on a style in the Styles Panel

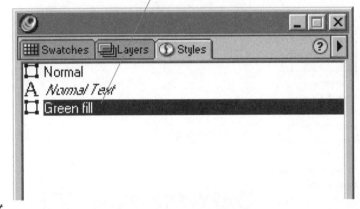

Text styles cannot be applied to objects. However, object styles can be applied to text — the fill and stroke of the object style is applied to the text box that appears behind the actual text itself.

3 The style is applied to the selected item

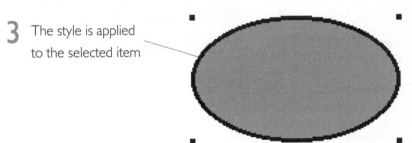

Dragging and dropping

To apply a style using drag and drop, an item does not have to be selected first. As long as the style is released over the required item, it will have that style applied to it.

1 Set the Styles Panel to preview mode (i.e. select Hide Names from the Styles Panel menu)

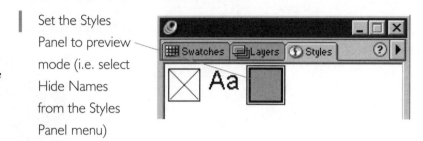

2 Click and drag a style until it is over the required item

To delete any styles that have been created but have not been used in a document select Remove Unused from the Styles menu. This should only be done if you are sure that you will not require the style in future and it is usually best to do this once you have completed an illustration.

3 Release the style. This will now be applied to the item it was dragged over

Styles can be exported and imported between documents in a similar way to symbols. See page 129 for more information about this.

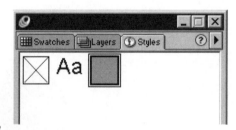

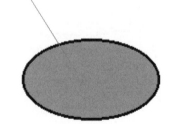

Working with text

In addition to working with graphics, Freehand also contains powerful features for adding text. This chapter looks at some of the options for adding and checking text and also some of the ways in which it can be manipulated.

Covers

Chapter Eight

Adding text

Text can be added to Freehand illustrations in a standard format, as with a word processing or desktop publishing program, or it can be given its own graphical effects. Text is added by using the Text tool and it can be done in two ways:

Both fixed-size and auto-expanding text boxes can be manipulated in the same way as other objects in terms of resizing.

Fixed-size

1 Select the Text tool from the Tools Panel and click and drag to create a fixed-size text box

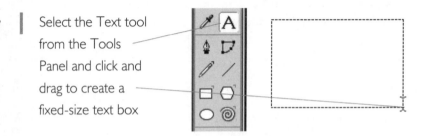

To split a single line of text in an auto-expanding text box, insert the Text tool at the point where you want the line to be split and press Return. This will contract the text box to the width of the longest line. However, if more text is then added, the text box will auto-expand again.

2 When text is added it will automatically 'wrap' when it gets to the end of the box

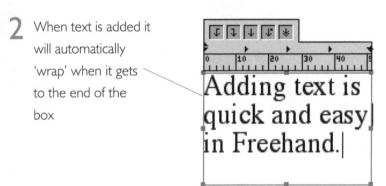

Auto-expanding

To display text block rulers, select View>Text Rulers from the menu bar.

1 Select the Text tool and click on a page. This creates an auto-expanding text box, which expands to accommodate any amount of text that is entered

Text Inspector

Once text has been added, it can be formatted using the Text Inspector.

To access the Text Inspector and its options:

 Text formatting options can also be selected in the Text Inspector before any text has been entered. These formatting options will then become the defaults for any new text that is entered. The default settings can only be changed if no text is currently selected.

1 Select Window>Inspectors>Text from the menu bar

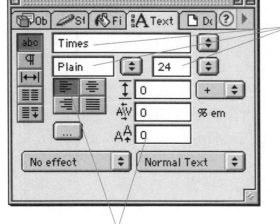

2 Click here to select font, size and formatting (bold or italic) options

 Spacing between lines is known as leading and spacing between letters is known as kerning. Both of these can be adjusted within the Text Inspector.

3 Select alignment and spacing options

 Once text has been added and the cursor is moved outside the text box, the cursor defaults to the Pointer tool. This can be changed by selecting Edit> Preferences, then clicking on the Text tab. Then check off the Text Tool Reverts to Pointer box.

4 Click here to select paragraph spacing and alignment options

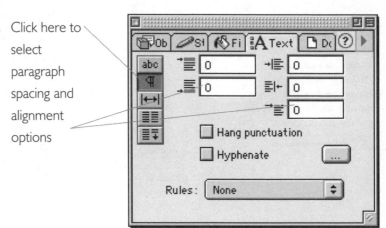

Selecting text

Text can be formatted by using the options in the Text Inspector, but it has to be selected first to do this. There are a number of ways to do this:

If a text block is selected, the formatting changes will be applied to all of the text within the block. If a single word, paragraph or range of text is selected, the formatting changes will only apply to these items.

Click once with the Pointer or Subselect tools to select a text block

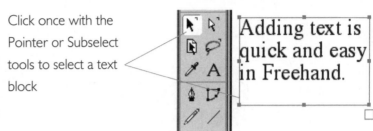

Click and drag with the Text tool to select a specific range of text

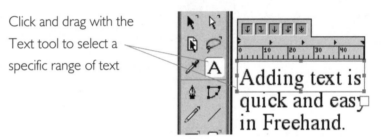

If a document with text blocks in it is saved as a Freehand file, the text blocks will still be fully editable the next time the file is opened. However, if the document has been exported into another format e.g. GIF or JPEG, the text will have become part of the image and will not be editable the next time it is opened in this format.

Double-click with the Text tool to select a single word

Triple-click with the Text tool to select a whole paragraph

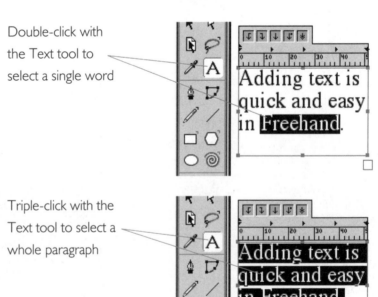

Text Editor

There may be occasions when you want to edit text outwith the normal authoring environment. This could be if the text contained non-printing characters or was formatted in an unusual way. In cases like this, the Text Editor could be used to display the text in a more manageable format and make editing easier. To use the Text Editor:

One use for the Text Editor is when text is contained within an envelope. For details about how to achieve this, see page 143.

I Select a text block with either the Pointer or Subselect tool

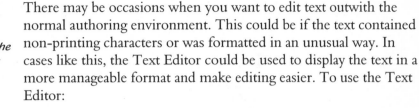

The Text menu also contains the same formatting options that appear in the Text Inspector.

2 Select Text>Editor from the menu bar

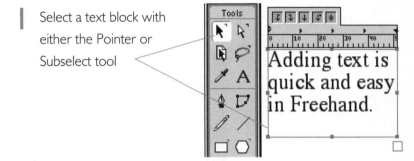

The main function of the Text Editor is to display text that could otherwise be difficult to edit.

3 Make editing changes in the Text Editor and select OK to apply them

Check on the Show Invisibles box in the Text Editor to display non-printing characters, such as paragraph breaks.

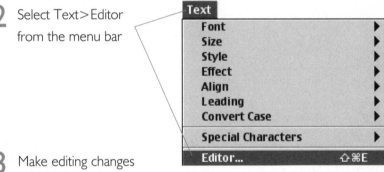

Find and Replace

Use the Find and Replace command to change words or phases within a text block:

1 Select a text block and select Edit>Find And Replace>Text from the menu bar

2 Enter the word or phrase to locate and what it should be changed to

The Find and Replace function can also be used to locate and alter a variety of attributes of graphical objects.

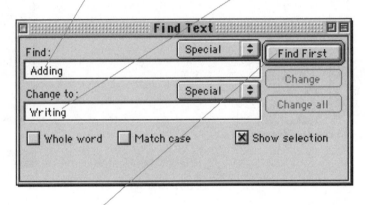

3 Select Find First and then (once the first occurrence of the word is found) Change or Change All

Once a word is found in the Find and Replace dialog box, select Change to replace each occurrence as it is found, or select Change All to change all occurrences automatically.

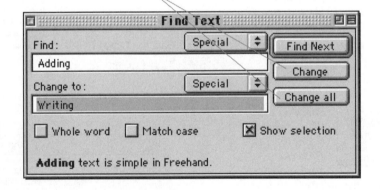

Checking spelling

Spelling can be checked in a similar way as using a spell checker in a word processing program.

To run a spell-check:

1 Select Text>
Spelling from the
menu bar

*The preferences
for the way the
Spelling dialog
box operates
can be set by
selecting Edit>Preferences
from the menu bar and then
selecting the Spelling tab
and clicking on the required
options.*

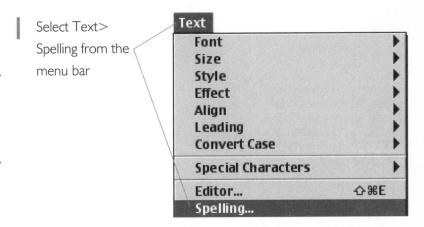

Text
Font ▶
Size ▶
Style ▶
Effect ▶
Align ▶
Leading ▶
Convert Case ▶
Special Characters ▶
Editor... ⇧⌘E
Spelling...

2 The spelling in all of the text blocks on the page will be checked in sequence. Select Ignore or Change for each word that is highlighted.

*When the
Spelling dialog
box highlights a
word that it
does not
recognise it provides an Add
button which can be used to
add the word to the custom
dictionary. If this is done,
the word will not be
highlighted the next time it
appears.*

Spelling

text

text
ext.
test
exit
taste

Ignore   Change
Ignore all Change all
Add   Suggest

UK English

☒ Show selection

Word found: **txt**
Writing txt is simple in Freehand.

Attaching text to paths

Text can be made to follow paths, in the same way as objects. This allows for considerable creative flexibility when combining text with graphics. To attach text to a path:

1 Create a path which the text will follow

When text has been attached to a path the Text Editor is a good option for editing the text.

Adding text to a path gives great effects

2 Create a text block and select both it and the path

The Object Inspector can be used to determine how the text follows the path to which it is attached. Use the options under Top, Bottom and Orientation to achieve this.

3 Select Text>Attach To Path from the menu bar

Text	
Font	▶
Size	▶
Style	▶
Effect	▶
Align	▶
Leading	▶
Convert Case	▶
Special Characters	▶
Editor...	⇧⌘E
Spelling...	
Run Around Selection...	⌥⌘W
Flow Inside Path	⇧⌘U
Attach To Path	⇧⌘Y

To release text from a path, select the path, then select Text>Detach from Path from the menu bar.

4 The text follows the path

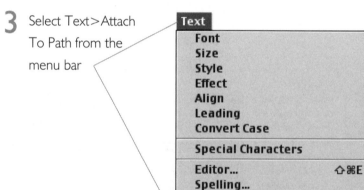

Text envelopes

Text envelopes can be used to create unusual formatting styles for text. It involves placing the text in a container that distorts the text to fit its own shape. To create a text envelope:

An envelope can also be applied to a selected text block by selecting Modify>Envelope>Create from the menu bar.

Use text envelope effects sparingly: as with many types of special effects, this can be irritating if it is overdone.

Text envelopes can be edited and manipulated in the same way as any other paths in Freehand. When a text envelope is manipulated the text within it is resized and reshaped, if necessary, to fit the new shape of the envelope.

1 Select a text block

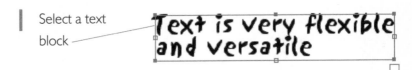

2 Select Window>Toolbars>Envelope from the menu bar

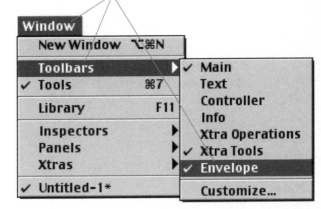

3 Click here to apply the current envelope style or click here to select a different one

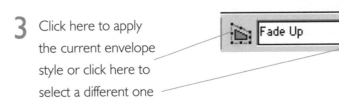

4 The text will be placed in the selected envelope style

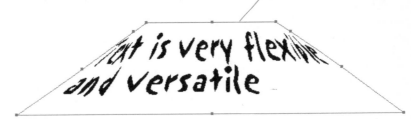

Text effects

From within the Text Inspector, an effects menu can be accessed to create a variety of text effects. To do this:

Text with effects applied takes up more file space than standard text without any effects.

1 Select a text box or highlight a piece of text

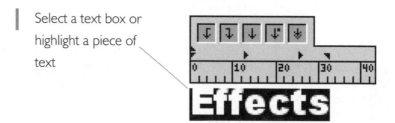

Some of the other buttons on the Text Inspector can be used to access options for highly specialised text formatting. These include:

- **Setting the distance between lines and letters;**
- **Hyphenation;**
- **Indents;**
- **Margins;**
- **Columns;**
- **Tables;**
- **Linking text blocks;**
- **Text wrapping and spacing options.**

There is insufficient space here to cover everything that can be done with text in Freehand but it is an extensive range that is comparable with a lot of word processing or desktop publishing programs.

2 Access the Text Inspector and click on this button, if it is not selected. Click here to access the Text Effects menu

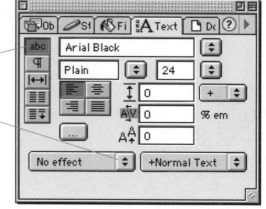

3 Select a text effect to apply to the text

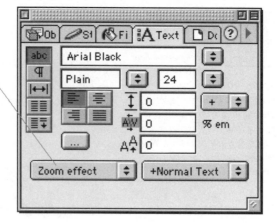

Samples of text effects

Highlight

Effects

Inline

Effects

Shadow

Effects

There is also a Graphic option on the Text Effect menu, but this is only applicable when used in conjunction with Inline, for the inclusion of inline graphics. This is an object that is inserted into a text block and can then be moved with the rest of the text.

Strikethrough

Effects

Underline

Effects

Zoom

Effects

Editing text effects

The only text effect that does not have editing options is the Shadow one.

Select the text with the effect applied to it and select Edit from the Text Effect menu. The related Edit dialog box will appear

Zoom Effect
Zoom To
80 %
Offset
x: 7.0555
y: 7.0555
From
Black
To
White
Cancel	OK

Paragraph styles

Paragraph styles can be created to define groups of formatting styles that can then be applied to a whole paragraph, in the same way as graphic styles can be applied to objects. To create a paragraph style:

Paragraph styles can be applied by inserting the cursor anywhere in a text block and selecting the required style from the Styles Panel. The paragraph in which the cursor is inserted will then take on the attributes of the selected style.

1 Select a text block and select Window>Panels>Styles from the menu bar

2 Click here and select New, then select the new style and select Edit

A new style is know as a child style, while the one on which it is based is known as the parent style.

To rename a paragraph style in the Styles Panel, select Edit>Show Names from the menu bar. Then double-click on the styles name and overtype a new one when it is highlighted.

3 Select a style on which you want the new one to be based and set the attributes that you want it to have. Select OK

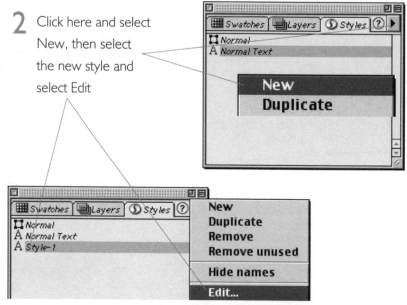

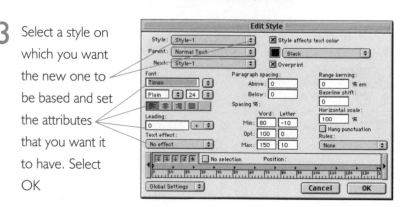

Web graphics

Freehand has the capacity for exporting graphics into a variety of formats, many of them for use on the web. This chapter looks at the process for achieving this and the formats that can be created. It also covers adding hyperlinks to files and creating and exporting animations.

Covers

Chapter Nine

About web graphics

Although Freehand is an excellent option for producing graphics for print, it also excels at creating ones that are ideal for use on web pages. In this respect files in the following formats can be created:

- JPEG

- GIF

- PNG

- PDF

In addition, the following formats can also be created:

JPEG, GIF and PDF are all image file formats that are designed primarily for use on the web. PDF is a format for converting items, while still retaining their original format. They can then be displayed using a variety of browsers or computer systems. This is a good option if there is a complex graphic which combines images and text.

- HTML. This is the format used for creating web pages and if pages are created in Freehand this way additional features can be added such as hyperlinks

- Flash SWF files. These are animated files that can be inserted into a web page

When graphics are produced in JPEG, GIF or PNG they are automatically compressed so that they can be downloaded as quickly as possible when they are viewed on the web. These are known as bitmap images, rather than vector ones, because they are made up of physical dots of colour rather than mathematical calculations, as with vectors.

Hyperlinks can also be inserted into SWF and PDF files.

JPEG images use up to 16 million colours and are ideal for photographs or gradients. GIF use 256 colours and are better suited to images with continuous tone colours. PNG is more similar to JPEG, but it has not become as widely accepted on the web.

Flash movies produced in SWF files are one of the most popular animation formats on the web. In order to view these files a plug-in Flash Player is required. This can be downloaded from the Macromedia website at www.macromedia.com and it is free of charge. In Freehand it is possible to preview Flash movies without having to first install the Flash Player.

Due to its versatility, Freehand is a excellent option for producing graphics for the web.

Exporting to JPEG, GIF and PNG

Before Freehand graphics can be used on the web, they have to be exported into a suitable format. For standard images this is either JPEG, GIF or PNG.

To export to JPEG, GIF or PNG:

If there is only a single object on the page, the export function will only create a JPEG, GIF or PNG of this object, regardless of how much space there is around it on the page. If there are two objects or more, the exported image will include the images and any space in between them.

1 Select File > Export from the menu bar

2 Select the required format

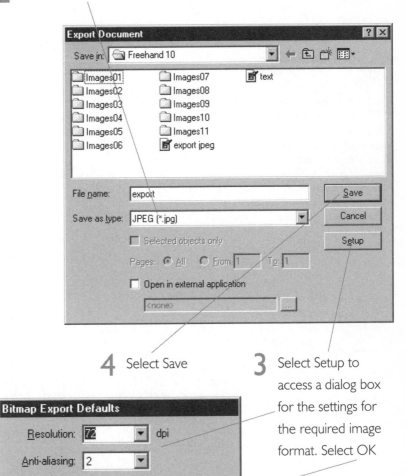

To only export one image from a complex graphic, select it first and then check on the Selected Objects Only box in the Export Document dialog box.

Check on the Open in External Application button to create an EXE file (i.e. a self-contained program that can be viewed on most devices and operating systems). However, this format is not suitable for inclusion in a web page.

4 Select Save

3 Select Setup to access a dialog box for the settings for the required image format. Select OK

Exporting to PDF

PDF (Portable Document Format) files are designed to be viewed on a variety of electronic devices and retain the exact format of the document from which they are created. However, they produce larger file sizes than JPEGs, GIFs of PNGs but are more versatile.

To export Freehand graphics in PDF:

In order to view PDF files, you need a plug-in called Adobe Acrobat Reader. This is free and can be accessed from the Adobe website at:

www.adobe.com

1 Select File>Export from the menu bar

2 Click here and select PDF

The options in the PDF Export dialog box include those for the way the colours are displayed, the version of the Acrobat Reader that the file is to be compatible with, and options for exporting miscellaneous items such as editable text, notes and URLs.

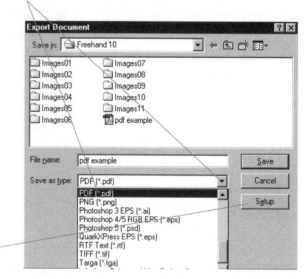

3 Select Setup

Unless it is specified to export a selected object to PDF, the whole page on which the objects are placed is converted. This can lead to unnecessary white space around the graphical elements.

4 Enter the required PDF settings and select OK. Select Save in the Export Document dialog box

Creating HTML

Although Freehand is by no means a web authoring program in the mould of Dreamweaver, it is still possible to create whole pages in HTML. This should not be used as an alternative to a dedicated web authoring program, but is can be useful for complex graphical pages that you do not want to have to export to an image and then import into another program.

If the default for exporting vector artwork (accessed by clicking the Setup button) is set to SWF, the Publish as HTML options creates an HTML file with the Freehand artwork inserted within it as a single image. It does not create HTML code for every single item on the page. So if you have included text, this will, in effect, be included in the image and so it will not be possible to edit this in a web authoring program.
However, if the default for exporting vector artwork is JPEG, GIF or PNG each object will be converted individually.

To create HTML files:

1 Select File > Publish as HTML from the menu bar

2 Click here to select HTML settings

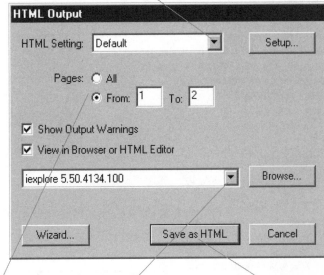

The Publish as HTML command relies heavily on the use of layers with the HTML document. This is a device for allowing different objects to overlap one another. The setting for these can be applied in the Setup dialog box or by using the Wizard. The Wizard also allows for a variety of other HTML options to be set.

3 Specify the pages that are to be converted to HTML

4 Click here to specify a default program for the HTML page (usually a browser or a web authoring program)

5 Select Save as HTML

Adding hyperlinks

For files that are going to be created in HTML, PDF or SWF it is possible to create hyperlinks for text or objects. In the published format, this appears as the link by which the user can jump to the related web page, or email address. Hyperlinks are created by adding URLs to objects or text. To do this:

URL stands for Uniform Resource Locator and it is the unique name of a website or email address.

1 Select an object or piece of text

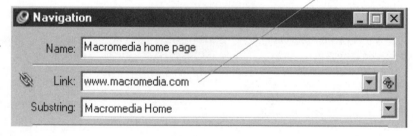

2 Select Window>Panels>Navigation from the menu bar

The Action, Events and Parameters boxes in the Navigation Panel are for URLs that have been added to files that are going to be exported into Flash SWF format.

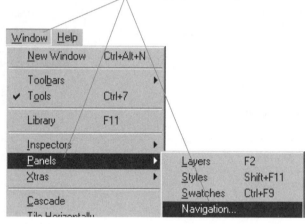

Once a hyperlink has been created to an object or a piece of text in a Freehand document, it has to be published into HTML or exported into PDF or SWF for the hyperlink to become active. This can be done by viewing the file in a browser. When the cursor passes over the element to which the hyperlink has been added, it will change into a pointing hand and if the element is clicked on it will take the user to the URL that has been included.

3 Enter a name for the hyperlink here (if required). Enter the URL here. Deselect the object to apply the hyperlink

Animating text

Both text and objects can be animated in Freehand and the result can then be exported as a Flash SWF file. Freehand also has a facility for viewing animations before they are exported. To create a text animation:

1   Select a text block

When text has been converted to paths, it takes on the properties of objects rather than text. The text cannot then be edited in the same way as before it was converted.

2   Select Text>
Convert to Paths
from the menu bar

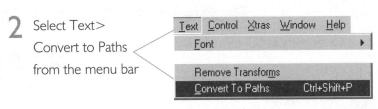

To copy and paste an object, select it, then select Edit>Copy from the menu bar, followed by Edit>Paste.

3   Select Modify>Join
from the menu bar

It is possible to move the start and end points of an animation even after it has been created.

4   Copy and paste the converted text block and drag it to where you want the animation to finish

...cont'd

Freehand creates animated effects by placing each element on a different layer and then displaying each layer in turn. It is similar to drawing an object on different pages of a book and then flicking through them to create an animated effect.

The animation options in the Release to Layers dialog box determine how the objects on each layer are displayed and the order in which the layers are displayed.

The Controller toolbar can be used to Play, Stop, Step Forwards or Step Backwards while an animation is previewing in the Flash Player. To access the Controller, select Window>Toolbars>Controller from the menu bar.

5 Select both pieces of text and select Xtras>Create>Blend from the menu bar

6 Select Xtras>Animate>Release to Layers from the menu bar

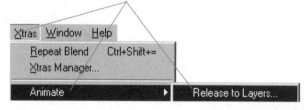

7 Select the animation options and select OK

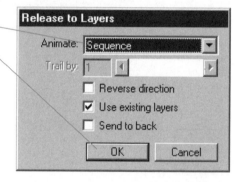

8 Select Control>Test Movie from the menu bar to preview the animation in the Flash Player

Animating objects

Objects can be animated just as effectively as text. However to do this, objects have to be either created as blends or as grouped objects. Once this has been done the object, or objects, can be animated:

To group objects, select them all (hold down Shift and click on all of the objects to be included in the group) and select Modify>Group from the menu bar.

1 Select the blend to be animated

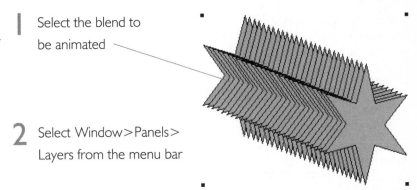

2 Select Window>Panels> Layers from the menu bar

When selecting options for an animation, note the following details:

- *Build creates an effect of the object being built on, while the objects on each layer are still visible;*

- *Sequence displays each layer in turn, without the others being in view;*

- *Drop creates an effect of the animate moving over all of the layers, and their content being visible;*

- *Trail is similar to Sequence except that the previous layers can be viewed as moving behind the currently visible one.*

3 Select Xtras>Animate>Release to Layers from the menu bar

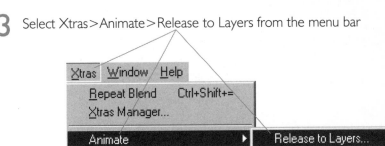

4 Select the required animation settings and select OK to animate the object

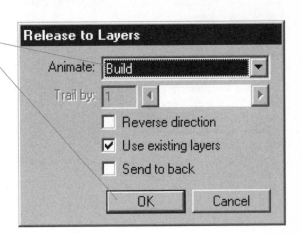

Animating different shapes

It is possible to create animations of one object transforming into another. This can also be done with text. This is sometimes known as morphing and it can be used to create striking animated effects.

To morph two different objects:

Objects with different fills can be blended and then animated, as well as those with different shapes.

Blending and animating objects in Freehand can create a smoother result than creating a similar effect in Flash. However, Flash has a greater flexibility for manipulating this type of animation once it has been created, so the best option could be to create it in Freehand and then export it into Flash. For details on how to do this, see page 158.

To create morphing effects between different numbers and letters, they have to first be converted into a suitable format. To do this, select the text and select Text>Convert to Paths from the menu bar. The text can then be animated in the same way as two different objects (see Steps 2–4).

1 Select two different objects

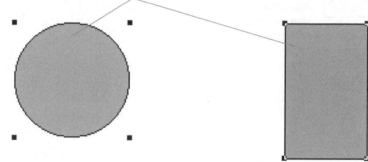

2 Select Xtras>Create>Blend from the menu bar

3 With the blend selected, select Xtras>Animate>Release to Layers from the menu bar

4 Set the animation settings as on the previous page, select OK and the blend will animate from one object to another

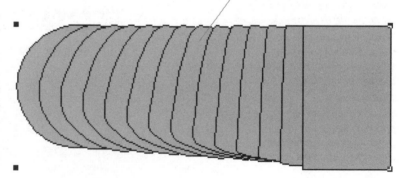

Previewing animations

Animated effects can be previewed in the Flash Player, that is installed when Freehand is first installed. This shows how the animation will play when it is viewed on a suitable browser. To preview an animation:

When animations are previewed they are done so in SWF files, which is the standard for displaying Flash movies.

1 Select Control> Test Movie from the menu bar

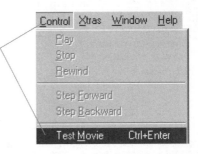

The Movie Settings dialog box can also be accessed by selecting Control>Movie Settings from the menu bar.

2 The animated effects are displayed here

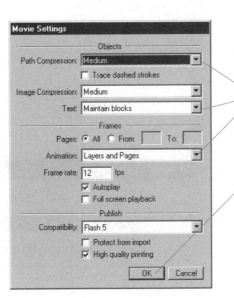

If the Movie Settings button is not visible, select Window> Toolbars> Controller from the menu bar. The Movie Settings button is located on this toolbar.

3 Click here to access the Movie Settings dialog box. Attributes can be set here for the way the movie is compressed and how it plays. Select OK to apply the settings

If more than one animation has been created on a page, they will play according to the layers on which they have been placed. This can be altered by changing the stacking order of the layers.

Exporting animations

In order for animations to be displayed properly they have to first be exported into a format that can easily be viewed on the web via a browser. In Freehand this means they are exported into the SWF format, which is the one used by the Flash Player. To export animations into this format:

Static graphics can be exported into the SWF format, but the main reason for exporting into this format is for animated graphics.

1 Select File>Export from the menu bar

2 Click here and select Macromedia Flash (SWF) here

The Flash Player plug-in is one of the most used ones on the Internet, with over 300 million downloads of it having taken place.

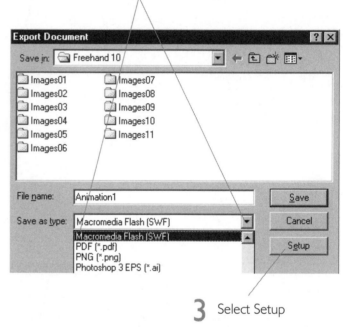

It is best to export each animated object separately. Then it is possible to incorporate them all, using the Flash program.

3 Select Setup

4 Specify how the file is to be compressed

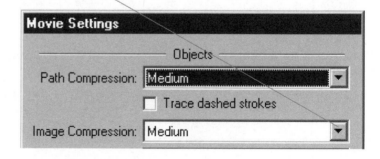

The more a file is compressed the faster it downloads in a browser. However, the quality can deteriorate. A balance should be struck between image quality and downloading time.

When SWF files are exported text can either be maintained in blocks or converted to paths.

The standard frames per second (fps) rate for animation playback over the web is 12.

If the Protect from import box is checked on, people viewing the file on the web will not be able to import the SWF file for their own use.

Once all of the animations settings have been selected, select OK in the Movie Settings dialog box to complete exporting the file.

5 Click here to select how text is exported

6 Select the pages to be exported

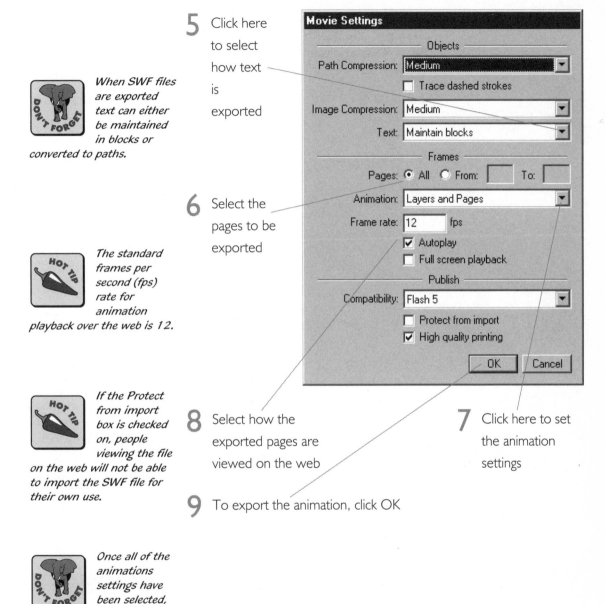

8 Select how the exported pages are viewed on the web

7 Click here to set the animation settings

9 To export the animation, click OK

Controller toolbar

The Controller toolbar can be used to provide shortcuts to testing and exporting movies and also to the Movie Settings dialog box. It can also be used to move through a movie when it is being previewed.

To access the Controller toolbar within a standard Freehand document:

1 Select Window>Toolbars>Controller from the menu bar

2 Only two options are available:

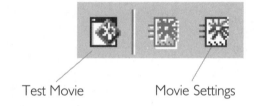

Test Movie   Movie Settings

The Controller toolbar is not visible when a movie is tested, unless it has already been accessed as in Step 1 on this page.

Test Movie

When a movie is being previewed as a result of selecting Test Movie, the rest of the Controller toolbar is available:

Stop   Step Backwards   Step Forwards   Export Movie

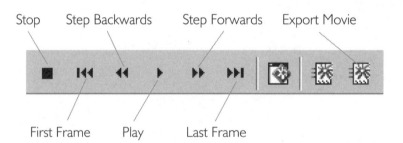

First Frame   Play   Last Frame

Xtras

Freehand offers an extensive range of options for manipulating and enhancing objects. These are known as Xtras and they can be used to create a variety of effects, such as embossing, roughening and 3D rotation. This chapter looks at the available Xtras and shows some of the effects that can be achieved, including the creation of charts.

Covers

Chapter Ten

About Xtras

Xtras are a group of options in Freehand that allow for some of the less straightforward aspects or functions of the program to be performed. Some of these, such as blends and animation, have been looked at in other chapters but there is still an extensive array of effects that can be accessed from within Xtras.

Xtra toolbars

There are two toolbars connected with Xtras that can be accessed from the menu bar, Operations and Tools:

Select Window>
Toolbars>Xtra
Operations (or
Xtra Tools)

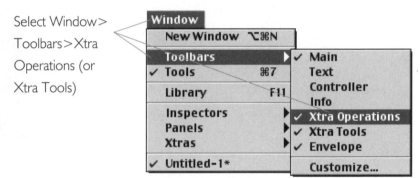

Xtra Operations Toolbar

Xtra Tools Toolbar

Xtra operations

Fractalize

This breaks objects up into smaller segments of the whole. To use the Fractalize tool:

The more times you click on an object, the more pronounced the Fractalized effect.

1 Select an object and click here on the Xtra Operations toolbar

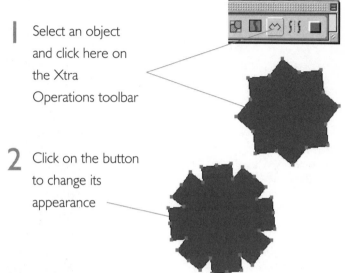

2 Click on the button to change its appearance

Trap

The Trap Xtra is a printing function that is used to avoid gaps of colour between two printed objects. To use the Trap tool:

If you are having a graphic printed commercially, ask your printer for details about the Trap setting that should be included.

1 Click here on the Xtra Operations toolbar

2 Enter the required Trap settings. Select OK

Trap

Trap width:

`0.0882`

☐ **Reverse traps**

— **Trap Color Method** —

○ **Use maximum value**

● **Use tint reduction**

Tint reduction: `40`

`Cancel` `OK`

Crop

This can be used to remove unwanted portions of bitmap images, but not vector ones. To use the Crop tool:

To crop an image proportionally, hold down Shift when the resizing handles are being dragged with the Crop tool.

The Transparency effect is dealt with in Chapter Five, page 94.

The Union, Divide, Punch and Intersect effects are dealt with in Chapter Five, pages 95–96.

1 Select a bitmap object and click here on the Xtra Operations toolbar

2 When the Crop cursor appears drag the resizing handles to crop the image

Other Xtras dealt with in other chapters

The Blend effect is looked at in Chapter Five, page 97.

Transparency		Punch	
Union		Intersect	
Divide		Blend	

Inset

This can be used to copy a smaller version of the selected object and place it inside the original. To use the Inset tool:

1 Select an object and click here on the Xtra Operations toolbar

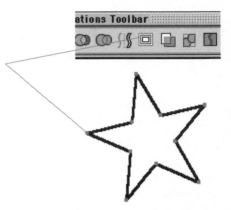

The Inset effect can be used in conjunction with other Xtras, such as Emboss, for an even more refined effect.

2 Enter the required values in the Inset Path dialog box. The higher the number of steps, the greater the number of insets that will appear

The Inset box in the Inset Path dialog box can be used to determine the distance between each occurrence of the object once they are inset into the original.

3 Select OK. The original object will appear with the designated number of insets inside it

Expand Stroke

This can be used to alter the size and properties of a selected path.

To use the Expand Stroke tool:

1 Select an path and click here on the Xtra Operations toolbar

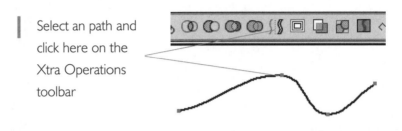

The Width box in the Expand Stroke dialog box determines the width of the selected stroke. This can be done by entering an exact value in the box, or by dragging the slider.

2 Enter the required values in the Expand Stroke dialog box

Similar results to those achieved with the Expand Stroke tool, can be achieved with the Stroke Inspector. This can be accessed by selecting Window>Inspectors>Stroke from the menu bar.

3 Select OK. The original object will be expanded according to the settings in Step 2

...cont'd

Remove Overlap

This can be used to remove unwanted path segments when two parts of the same path overlap one another. Instead, a composite path is created that amalgamates the overlapping sections. To use the Remove Overlap tool:

1 Select an overlapping path and click here on the Xtra Operations toolbar

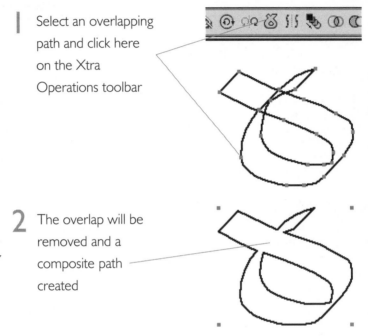

If the Reverse Direction command is applied to a single path, this alters the items such as the resizing handles and any arrowheads that are being used.

2 The overlap will be removed and a composite path created

Reverse Direction/Correct Direction

These can be used to alter how the fills of composite paths are displayed. To use these tools:

Composite paths can be created when two paths are touching each other. To do this, select Modify>Join from the menu bar.

Select a composite path and click here on the Xtra Operations toolbar

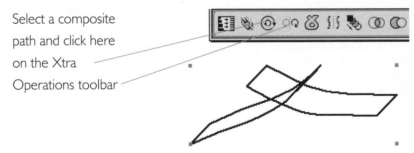

Emboss

This can be used to give objects the appearance of having a raised, or sunken surface. To use the Emboss tool:

 *The Navigation and Release to Layers options are looked at in greater detail in Chapter Nine.*

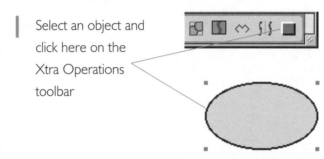

1 Select an object and click here on the Xtra Operations toolbar

 Embossing is a good option for creating items such as buttons for web pages.

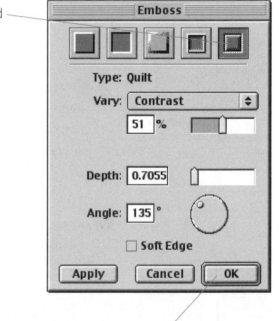

2 Select the required embossing effects

 *Experiment with embossing effects to see which ones are best for different purposes.*

 The final item on the Xtra Operations toolbar is the Add Points tool. This is similar to the Simplify tool, except that it adds points to a path instead of removing them. This can be useful for precise editing of a path. Each time this tool is clicked, more points are added to a selected path.

3 Select OK and view the selected effect

Xtra tools

Arc

As its name suggests, the Arc tool is used to create arcs:

Once an arc has been created with the Arc tool, it can be manipulated in the same way as any other path.

Select the Arc tool and click and drag to create an arc on the page. This is a path with two points, one at either end of the arc

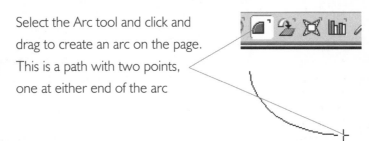

Some interesting effects can be achieved with the Fisheye Lens tool if it is applied to photographic images.

Fisheye Lens

This can be used to create a fisheye effect. This is a common photographic technique where an image appears to be concave or convex. To use the Fisheye Lens tool:

Double-click the Fisheye Lens tool to access its dialog box. This can be used to determine the shape of the effect and whether it is concave or convex.

1 Select an object and click here on the Xtra Tools toolbar

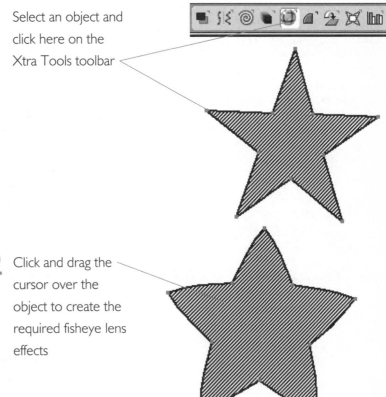

The Fisheye Lens tool can be applied to whole objects or just parts of them.

2 Click and drag the cursor over the object to create the required fisheye lens effects

...cont'd

3D Rotation

This can be used to rotate two-dimensional objects so that they take on a 3D effect. To use the 3D Rotation tool:

The Rotate From options in the 3D Rotation dialog box determine the point around which the object will be rotated. These are:

- *Mouse click, which is the point where you click on the page;*
- *Center of selection, which is the centre of the object;*
- *Center of gravity, which is the visual centre of the object;*
- *Origin, which is the bottom left-hand corner of the object.*

The tool next to the 3D Rotation tool is the Spiral tool. This is looked at in Chapter Three, page 59.

1 Select an object and double-click on the 3D Rotation button on the Xtra Tools toolbar

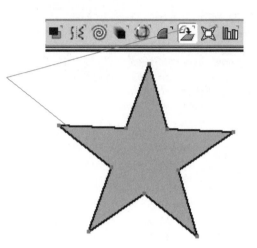

2 Select the settings for the rotation in the 3D Rotation dialog box

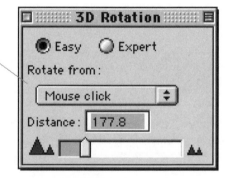

3 Click and drag to rotate the object and give it a 3D effect

Smudge

This creates a smudged effect around the edge of an object. To use the Smudge tool:

Double-click the Smudge tool to access the Smudge dialog box. This offers options for the colour of the smudged effect. Drag the required colour from the Swatches Panel and the smudge effect will take on the appearance of a shaded version of this colour.

1 Select an object and click here on the Xtra Tools toolbar

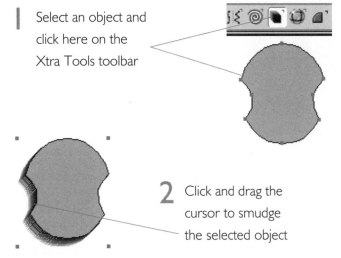

The Smudge tool can be applied to text, but it has to be first selected and then the Release to Layers command applied to it.

2 Click and drag the cursor to smudge the selected object

Eyedropper

This can be used to copy a colour from one object to another. To use the Eyedropper tool:

1 Click here on the Xtra Tools toolbar

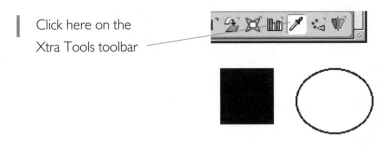

The Eyedropper tool is also available on the Tools Panel.

2 Click on a colour and drag it to another object to apply it to that one

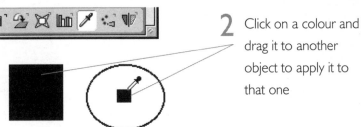

Shadow

This can be used to create a shadow effect behind a selected object. It is similar to the Drop Shadow function that some programs have, but it offers more flexibility. To use the Shadow tool:

In the Shadow dialog box, the Fill options determine the colour and density of the shadow and the Scale option determines its size, as a percentage of the original object.

When creating a shadow effect, an outline appears when you click and drag the selected object. This is the outline of the shadow and where this is moved to is where the shadow effect will be placed.

Keep shadows near to the original object for a subtle effect. Place them further away, and at a scale size of over 100%, for a more dramatic effect.

1 Select an object and double-click here on the Xtra Tools toolbar

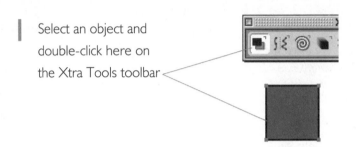

2 Select the settings for the shadow effect in the Shadow dialog box. Select OK to apply the shadow

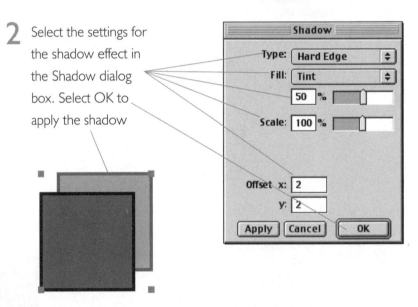

3 Click and drag on the selected object to change the position of the shadow

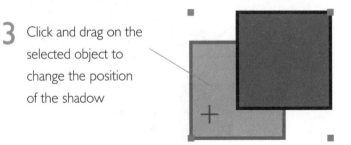

Roughen

This can be used to create a jagged effect along previously smooth paths. To use the Roughen tool:

If an object has already had an effect such as Shadow applied to it, this will become jagged too when the Roughen tool is applied.

1 Select an object and click here on the Xtra Tools toolbar

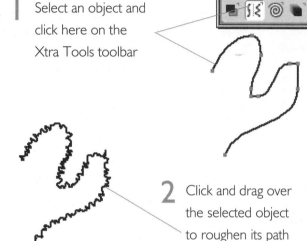

Double-click on the Roughen tool to access its dialog box. This can be used to specify the amount that an object is to be roughened by and whether the edges are rough or smooth.

2 Click and drag over the selected object to roughen its path

Bend

This can be used to bend all sides of an object simultaneously. To use the Bend tool:

The tool next to the Roughen tool is the Mirror tool. This is similar to the Reflect tool on the Tools Panel, which is looked at in Chapter Five, page 91.

1 Select an object and click here on the Xtra Tools toolbar

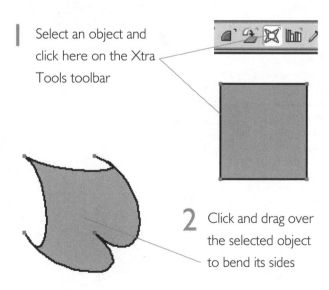

2 Click and drag over the selected object to bend its sides

Graphic Hose

This can be used to spray numerous copies of an object onto a page in quick succession. Up to 10 objects can be included in each hose, in which case they are inserted in sequence. Alternatively, a hose could consist of one object and this can be sprayed as frequently as required. Hoses are Freehand files that contain objects that are replicated on the page when the Graphic Hose tool is activated. There are some hoses that are already created within the program, while new ones can also be created. To use the Graphic Hose tool:

Click once to add a single object with the Graphic Hose, rather than spraying several by dragging.

1 Double-click here to access the Graphic Hose tool and its dialog box

To delete an object from a hose group, select it in the Contents box and click on delete.

2 Click here and select a Freehand file that will perform as the hose. Click here to see the items contained in the file

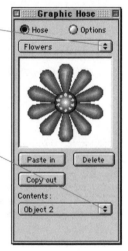

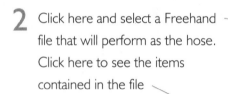

Use the Up and Down arrows while dragging to increase or decrease the scale between objects. Use the Left and Right arrows to increase or decrease the spacing between objects

3 Click and drag to spray the hose on the page

...cont'd

A variety of objects can be included in a Graphic Hose, including bitmaps, groups, blends and text.

Select the Options button in the Hose dialog box to access options for the way the Graphic Hose operates. These include: Order, Spacing, Scale and Rotate.

If you want to include numerous objects within a Graphic Hose, create them separately and then follow Steps 3 and 4 for each individual item.

Use the Copy Out button in the hose dialog box to copy the selected object onto the Clipboard so that it can be pasted into a document as a single object.

To create a new Graphic Hose:

1 Double-click the Graphic Hose button on the Xtra Tools toolbar. In the Hose dialog box, click here and select New

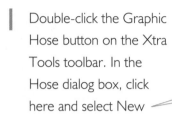

2 Enter a name for the new Graphic Hose and select Save

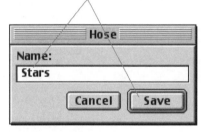

3 Create the required content, select it and select Edit>Copy from the menu bar

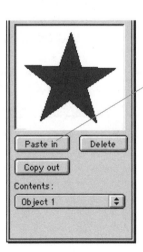

4 In the Hose dialog box, select Paste in to include the object in the selected Graphic Hose

Xtras menu

The Xtras menu can be accessed from the menu bar and contains a number of submenus:

The final tool on the Xtra Tools toolbar is the Chart tool. This also appears on the Xtras menu and is looked at in greater detail on pages 177–180.

1 Select Xtras from the menu bar. This displays the main Xtras menus

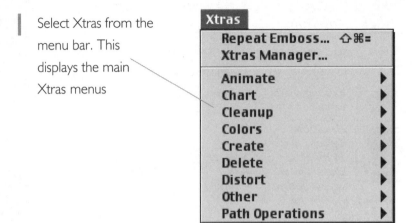

2 Click on a heading to view its submenu

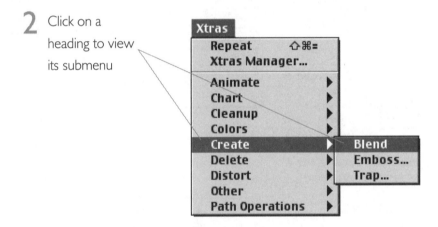

Most of the options found on the Xtras menu can be accessed from other parts of Freehand, such as the Xtra Tools toolbar or the Xtra Operations toolbar. It is a matter of individual preference as to how these items are accessed.

Creating charts

Freehand not only provides the tools for creating original artwork, it also has a function for creating charts and graphs. These can then be exported and used in other documents for presentations or reports. Charts and graphs are created by using the Chart button on the Xtra Tools toolbar:

Existing charts can also be edited by selecting Xtra> Chart from the menu bar.

1 Click here on the Xtra Tools toolbar

2 Click and drag the cursor to create the required size of the chart

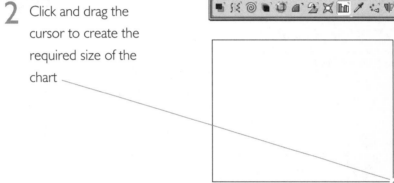

The value in the Decimal Precision box, determines the number of decimal points that are applied to each number. This value affects all of the numbers in the table; you cannot apply different levels of precision to different numbers.

3 In the Chart dialog box, enter the data that will be included in the chart

After each item of data has been entered, click on Apply or another cell in the table to insert the data into the table.

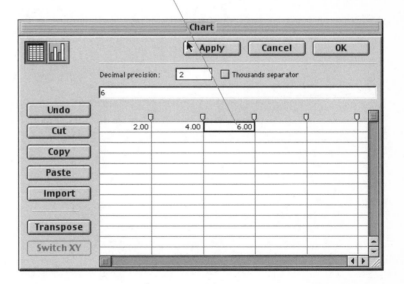

4 The chart is
displayed in the
document window

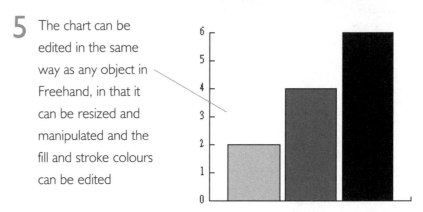

5 The chart can be
edited in the same
way as any object in
Freehand, in that it
can be resized and
manipulated and the
fill and stroke colours
can be edited

6 With the chart still selected, double-click on the Chart button to
return to the Chart dialog box and amend the data as required

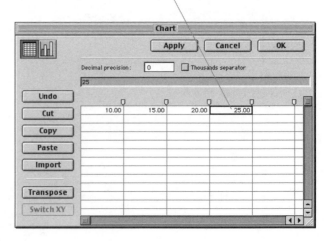

Editing charts

The way a chart is presented can be edited, to include legends and different formats for items such as the x- and y-axis. To do this:

1 Select a chart and double-click the Chart button

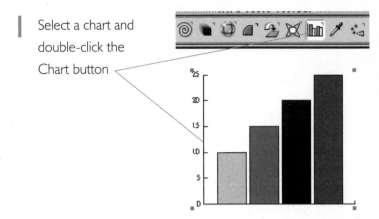

To create a legend (the labels that define each bar in the chart) type a textual name in the cells in the Chart dialog box before the numerical data is added. Enter this in the cells below each of the relevant titles.

2 Click here to access the chart formatting options

Enter values here or drag the slider to determine the width of columns in the chart

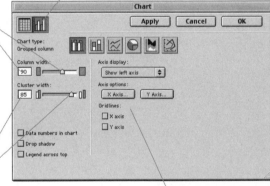

Tick the boxes in the bottom left-hand corner of the dialog to determine:

- Whether numbers are displayed at the top of each column;
- Drop shadows are included for each data bar;
- Whether the legend appears along the top or side of the chart.

Enter values here or drag the slider to determine the distance between columns in the chart

Specify how the x- and y-axis are displayed and whether they display gridlines

Chart formats

Using the Chart dialog box, charts can be displayed in several different styles:

Select a chart and click here in the Chart dialog box and select a style

Each different chart type has its own options for formatting. These become available once each chart type has been selected.

Available styles

Grouped columns

Stacked columns

Line

Pie

Area

Scatter

Printing

Printing documents in Freehand can be straightforward or it can be a complex commercial process. This chapter gives an overview of the printing process and shows how to set up documents ready for printing.

Covers

Chapter Eleven

Print settings

Freehand is designed to give optimum results, regardless of whether items are intended for display on the web or for hardcopy publishing. There are a range of options that can be accessed when printing graphic documents and these can be used for a home or small-office printer, or for a high quality commercial one. For the former, an inkjet desktop printer will usually suffice, but if a commercial printer is being used then the document should be prepared for printing on a high resolution PostScript device.

Whichever output device you are going to use, the print settings can still be specified before the document is actually printed. To do this:

Non-PostScript printer

PostScript is a format for printing high quality documents. It refers to the format of the document rather than just the type of printer. If a PostScript printer is being used by a commercial printer then they will require the file to be saved into the PostScript format.

1 Select File>Print from the menu bar

All Print dialog boxes differ as they have options that are specific to the selected printer. The general items that will be available are:

- *Page range;*
- *Number of copies;*
- *Page orientation;*
- *Colour management;*
- *Scaling*

Check the printer's documentation for the complete range of print options.

2 Select the non-PostScript printer and select the required print options

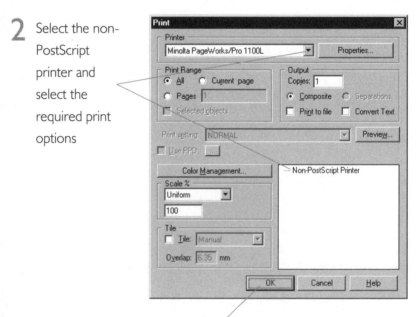

3 Select OK (Windows) or Print (Mac) to print the document

PostScript printer

1 Select File>Print from the menu bar

2 Select the PostScript printer and select the required print options.

Click on the Properties button to access additional settings for the printed document. This applies equally to PostScript and non-PostScript printers (although the properties will be specific to the selected printer).

For PostScript printing, the best results are achieved when the printer's matching PostScript Printer Description (PPD) file is selected. This contains information that ensures that the settings for the selected printer are optimised. To select a PPD file, check on the PPD box in the Print dialog box. Navigate to the required file (the correct folder should be opened automatically), select it and select Open.

3 Select OK (Windows) or Print (Mac) to print the document

Additional PostScript options are available here

Print Preview

When printing illustrations, it is useful to be able to preview what the finished version will look like when it is printed. This gives an overview of the whole page and it can save valuable time and printer consumables if there is a mistake that requires to be corrected or the layout does not look quite right.

To use Print Preview:

For both Windows and Mac the Setup button can be used to access the Print Preview dialog box for PostScript printers.

1 Select File>Print from the menu bar

2 For non-PostScript printers, select Preview (Windows) or Setup (Mac)

PostScript printers tend to have a wider range of Print Preview options than non-PostScript ones.

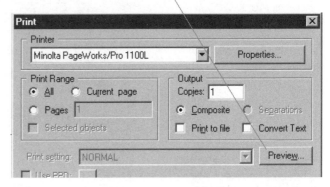

If a document consists of more than one page, the Print Preview dialog box can be used to move through all of the pages and see how they will all print.

3 The Print Preview dialog box shows how the illustration will be printed and how close to the edge an item can be for it to be included in the printed output

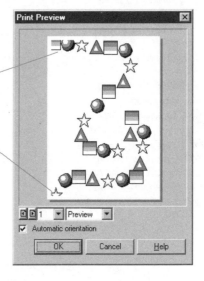

If you are using screened objects in a document, halftone settings can be used to determine the way they print. To do this, select Window>Panels>Halftones from the menu bar.

Print Area

The Print Area option can be used to select a specific area of the page for printing. Once this has been done, the rest of the page will be ignored by the printer. To set a Print Area:

The Print Area tool can also be accessed by selecting File>Print Area from the menu bar.

1 Click here on the main toolbar

2 Click and drag to select the required Print Area

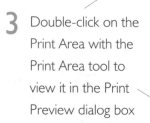

The area displayed by a Print Area box can be altered by moving the cursor over the border of the box until it changes into a clenched hand. Then drag the Print Area box to a new location. This then changes the display in the Print Preview dialog box.

3 Double-click on the Print Area with the Print Area tool to view it in the Print Preview dialog box

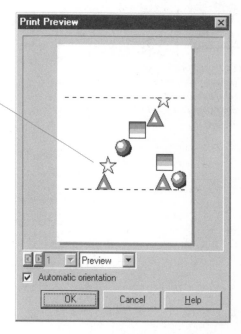

Print Area boxes can also be resized by clicking and dragging on their borders.

Document reports

If you are using a commercial printer for your final artwork it will benefit all concerned if you can give them as much information as possible about the items to be printed. This can be done by producing a document report:

If in doubt about what to include in a report, select all of the options and print reports on them all. If you miss one, this will probably be the one that the printer requires. It is always worth checking with the printer to find out exactly what it is they want from you.

1 Select File>Report from the menu bar

2 Check on the boxes for the categories to be reported on. Select OK

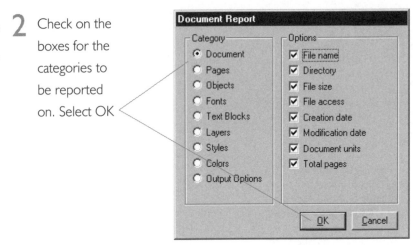

High quality printing can be a complex business and it is always best to consult professional printers for their specific requirements, if you are going to be using their services.

3 The report is created for the items selected in Step 2. Scroll down here to see the full report

4 Select Print to create a hard copy

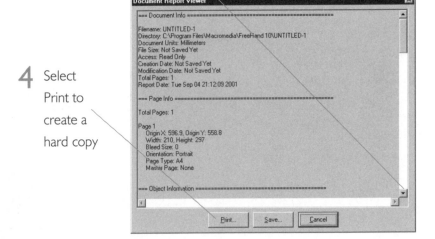

Index

A

Add Points button   74
Adobe
   Illustrator   53
Align Panel. *See* Panels: Align
Aligning   92
Animations
   Animating different shapes   156
   Animating objects   155
   Animating text   153–154
   Controller toolbar   160
   Exporting   158–159
   Movie settings   157
   Previewing   157
   Release to Layers   154
Arrange command   93
AutoCad DXF   53

B

Bitmaps   53, 99
Bleed settings. *See* Inspectors: Document: Bleed settings
Blends
   Creating   97
   Joining to paths   98

C

Charts
   Creating   177–178
   Editing   178–179

Formats   180
   Ungrouping   178
Children   128, 146
Circles
   Drawing   58
Color Mixer Panel. *See* Panels: Color Mixer
Colours
   Adding   105–106
   Applying   109
      Via the Fill Inspector   110–111
      Via the Fill Panel   112–115
   Creating   103–104
   Deleting   107
   Editing   107–108
   Getting information about   102
   Naming   107
   Xtras colour options   108
Custom fills   111

D

Document Inspector. *See* Inspectors: Document
Documents
   Creating   26
   Printing. *See* Printing
   Reports
      Creating   186
   Setup   26
Dreamweaver. *See* Macromedia: Dreamweaver

E

Ellipses
   Drawing   58
Encapsulated PostScript. *See* EPS
Enhanced Metafiles   53
EPS   52–53
Exporting. *See* Files: Exporting

F

G

H

I

R

S

T